CHRISTOP

Right voices, Right choices

CLICKBAIT

WIN THE WAR FOR YOUR MIND IN THE AGE OF DISTRACTION

CLICKBAIT

ISBN: 978-1-955362-07-8

Although both the publisher and author have used reasonable care in preparing this book, the information it contains is distributed "as is" and without warranties of any kind. This book is not intended as legal, financial, or health advice, and not all the recommendations will be suitable for your situation. Professional legal, financial, and professional health advisors should be consulted, as needed. Neither the publisher nor the author shall be liable for any costs, expenses, or damages resulting from the use of or reliance on the information contained in this book.

Published by
STORY CHORUS

PRAISE FOR *CLICKBAIT*

"Chris has proven himself to be a voice of truth that is here to stay. If *Up Next* was a handbook on leadership, *Clickbait* is a survival strategy for spiritual success in a climate geared toward our failure. Chris takes the complex truth of silencing the negative voices demanding our attention, and he makes it clear how vital it is to have true focus in our lives. I am grateful for his impact and his friendship. I trust that *Clickbait* will provide you with the kind of encouragement you need to persevere!"

Justin McNeil
Associate Pastor at City of Life Church

"There's many distractions keeping us away from God's plan and purpose for our lives. *Clickbait* is a powerful tool for identifying the tactics of the enemy and empowering us to lead strong in the kingdom of God. Chris's biblical insight and stories of faith will inspire you to lead and live better; they have done as much for me."

Dan Rivera
Pastor, Songwriter, and Worship Artist

"Clickbait is a real issue. You can get angry or you can get educated. Every believer needs to read this book! This book by Chris Alessi will uncover the enemy's lies, give you insight to the "hooks" of spiritual clickbait, and give you a real strategy to overcome distractions so you can move into your future!"

Martha Munizzi
Pastor and Gospel Artist

"*ClickBait* is an 'in your face' book that packs a punch and cuts right to today's issues that the enemy uses to take us out. In this book, Chris breaks down the four voices that we all listen to and reveals that the clickbait voice deals the most lethal blow, and how it's suffocating us on a daily basis. Thankfully, *ClickBait* gives us the tools to fight and the specific 'how-to's' to confront these tactics that are trying to keep us in isolation and destroy our marriages, relationships, and families."

Doug Wood
Author of *Church Boy to Millionaire*

"Chris has taken a relevant concept called 'clickbait' and pulled me into the reality of how we rise or fall with our thought life. As I began to mine through the pages, I could instantly see myself: the times I had to make pivotal decisions that could lead me forward or derail me from my destiny. Every one of those decisions were made in my thought life. But clickbait was always there trying to lure me away with subtle distractions. This book is an excellent tool to help shape our ability to see rightly and to listen to the right voices. Don't fall for clickbait."

David Binion
Lead Pastor at Dwell Church

"Chris consistently proves to be a voice to multiple generations. This book is exceptionally relevant and surgically insightful. The practical elements presented in *Clickbait* for recognizing the distractions that are thrown at us and how to combat them on a daily basis are invaluable. There are winning formulas in these pages. Grab the gold that is presented and watch the wins pile up."

Chris Hart
CEO of The Brave Group, Bear Grip Inc., & The Momentum Collective

"Distractions can be deadly. How many times have we dangerously and unknowingly veered too close to the edge all because we took the bait? As a minister and leader for 30 years, this is one of the most profound writings on how we fall prey to clickbait. Chris's book is destined to be a treasure of truth for anyone who reads it. At a time when we may worry about the depth of the future generation, this book proves we are in capable hands. I am so grateful to God that the writer, who just happens to be my son, is willing to step out and expose the enemy's tactics. Go get 'em Chris."

Mary Alessi
Pastor at Metro Life Church & Gospel Artist

TO PAPA,

THANK YOU FOR THE LEGACY OF LIFE AND MINISTRY.

REST EASY.

CONTENTS

PART 3: THE SOLUTION

FOREWORD

Whether it's my age or because I don't care for social media all that much, I never understood what "clickbait" was. Quite frankly, I didn't care. But I remember the day I found out.

I was about four clicks into a post with a headline that read: "These people didn't realize this would be in the background of their picture!"

I couldn't wait to see the humor in these pictures. So I clicked on the image... which then took me to another image... which took me to another one! Then it hit me: none of the images I looked at matched the first one that promised something truly crazy. Instead, I spent way too much time (time I would never get back) searching for something that was fake.

When I got over the annoyance of feeling suckered, I realized that's what clickbait is. Clickbait is a false advertisement that draws us in with the promise of something great but offers zero of that promised value.

I've experienced this phenomenon many times in life, and I'm sure you have, too. But internet clickbait is hardly a worry compared to the minefield lurking just underfoot in our everyday thought lives.

After more than thirty years of pastoral ministry, I know firsthand how often people make decisions when they agree with a thought. And sometimes, sadly, those thoughts are misleading half-truths or even outright lies. We've all bought into the advertisement only to feel let down when it was all over.

Could it be a relationship? Maybe a career move? Possibly your identity? Or perhaps something else entirely you are grappling with right now? Regardless of where you've been, or even where you are at today, this book will help you navigate the many “clickbaits” that plague our lives. Read on to understand the nature of the war and be equipped for the battle each and every day.

Steve Alessi
Founder and Lead Pastor, Metro Life Church

TERMS & CONDITIONS (AKA: SKIP THIS PART)

One of the biggest hindrances to actually sitting and finishing this book has been Instagram's Popular page. Every time I sit down to write, I open up Instagram instead and mindlessly scroll. Each still image somehow grips my attention, and I lose thirty minutes before I even realize it.

Everything I see is both amazing and completely unnecessary, and I get angry—not only with myself for wasting time, but with every single content uploader on my Popular page. They purposefully captioned or edited the image to make me believe something truly life-changing was on the other end of that click, and I'm the sucker that fell for it. Like the girl who posted "My starbucks stalker," only for me to discover the barista simply read her name off the cup. Or the countless "wait for it" videos that don't have anything worth waiting for. I keep getting sucked into images of my favorite professional athletes with the words "Breaking News" over them, only to find out it's a sports parody page and there is no real breaking news.

I click each link under the promise of something truly life-changing, just to leave disappointed. There might be cool stuff, but nothing ever seems to match the caption. The content never lives up to the promise. That's just the norm these days.

It seems impossible to go through our social world without being bombarded by headlines that radicalize, overpromise, and even flat-out lie! Every video is of some random person with an agenda claiming to destroy another person with an agenda. Every article holds the promise of some shocking revelation.

In short, we've been ravaged by clickbait culture, which has made it hard to find anything of value on the internet. Our clicks have become just as valuable as our dollars, and so companies and content creators do whatever they can to get us to click. It's kind of funny really! Most of their promises don't ever live up to the hype, and yet we keep on clicking.

As funny and lighthearted as most clickbait is, some of it is downright misleading, and some of it is just lies. People use this type of clickbait to anger and divide us. This type of clickbait has overvalued debate and destroyed conversation.

I hope books will be written on the clickbait culture we live in and the very real effects it's having on our day-to-day life, but that won't be this book. I intend to use clickbait to paint a picture of the even more real mental battle in the life of a Christian, the twelve-round, seemingly never-ending battle for your attention and ultimately your faith.

Just like the Popular page, you are being bombarded with accusation after accusation, threat after threat, on a daily basis. You are fighting off an enemy that is seeking to kill, steal, and destroy, all while going to school, work, leading a family, and enjoying your time under the sun. Waves of negative emotion, guilt, and shame overtake you as you wage war in a battle that isn't flesh and blood.

I've been a Christian for thirty years now. I was one of those lucky kids who was born into Christianity. I've never spent a day outside of a relationship with God! I did, however, make the personal decision to be a Christian when I was around thirteen. I felt called to the ministry when I was nineteen. So now that I'm seventeen years into my personal relationship with Christ, I find myself pondering some very serious questions. Why do I struggle so much? As a pastor who truly believes the Word of God to my core, why is it still hard? I'm a seven on the Enneagram, the life of the party, and yet my biggest battle is keeping that party going when it's just me, myself, and I.

I know I'm not the only one. Why do Christians struggle so much? Why are so many of us anxious, depressed, bitter, or tired? Why are so many of us struggling with self-confidence? How can those of us that know the truth live such similar lives to those that don't know the truth? How is it that we know the enemy is a liar but still struggle with what he says?

It's not just us. Have you ever thought about why the people in the Bible struggled the way they did too? Why did Eve eat the fruit? How could Sarai laugh? Why couldn't the other ten spies see past the giants? Why did Aaron let the Israelites build a golden calf? Why were Shadrach, Meshach, and Abednego the only ones to not bow? Why did Thomas struggle to believe before he saw?

These are the types of questions that we will wrestle with in this book, and each one is complex. But there is a simple answer: from the beginning of time until now, each one of us has to fight our very own battle with the enemy's clickbait.

We have a very real enemy hurling insults and accusations at us every chance he gets to see what sticks. He's a master of his craft, using these weapons as clickbait to get us into dialogue with him. Once that happens, it's all she wrote. The fat lady has started warming up. In his sermon, "Words to Live By," Pastor Craig Groeshel says, "Life moves in the direction of your strongest thoughts." If our enemy can get us to think the wrong thoughts, we're well on our way to living the wrong life.

But it doesn't have to be this way. You can fight back and let God fight for you! You can be happy, healthy, and whole. You can think thoughts that help and don't hinder you. You can lead a family, run at giants, and take the Gospel to the nations. You can walk in everything God has made available for His people. You can do this and so much more! You've already taken a step in that direction by not only buying this book, but also by choosing to read it.

We will spotlight a few of the enemy's clickbait tactics and introduce some tools to help you fight off each one. We will look at the seemingly harmless thoughts we all think, which we've all called "normal," and look at the very real effects they can have on us. This battle with the enemy's clickbait may not be one we can win outright, but it's one we can manage. The Bible is filled with people who had low points, who maybe lost a round or two, but they came out on top. You will come out on top too!

PART 1

THE PROBLEM

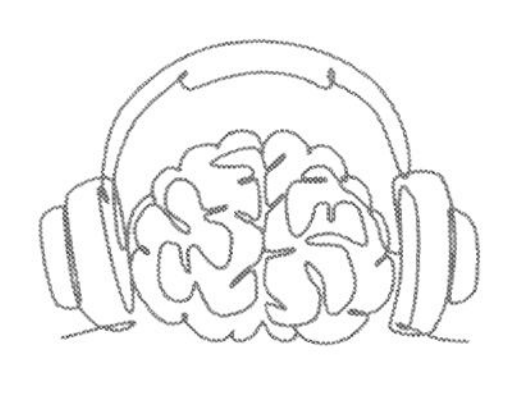

CHAPTER 1

LOCATION SERVICES

I can envision some influencer trying to caption the last scene of humanity's season of perfection with, "what happens next is truly unbelievable! No, really!" Their camera phone pans through a beautiful garden to find an unclothed woman talking to a talking serpent. It's an influencer's goldmine! If someone was able to livestream the opening moments of Genesis 3, there would be reaction videos all over the internet! It would be the subject of every podcast, every late-night talk show, and the meme pages would have a field day!

I wouldn't be able to blame them though. The scene of Genesis 3 is awkwardly set! No matter how weird the picture is though, I don't think anyone would have realized that the state of the world was at the mercy of this conversation. I can imagine the livestreamer fumbling to stop the stream as they hear God searching for them. It went from zero to 100 *real* quick! It was the world's first, "That Escalated Quickly."

The escalation was real. The serpent asks Eve if God really said they would die one moment, and God is asking them where they are the next. From walking in the cool of the day together, to God cutting them out of the garden for their own protection. From one minute to the next, Adam and Eve went from perfection in the garden with God to banished and seemingly on their own.

It's easy to say that this story explains what *happened* to humanity, but I think it's just as fair to say it describes what is currently *happening* as well. When we look at the state of Christians and non-Christians alike, I don't think it's a stretch to say that God is still wondering where we are.

God asking, "Where are you?" in verse nine of Genesis 3 carries significant implications, both for then and for now.

This was the all-seeing, all-knowing, personal God who would walk in the cool of the day with them. He formed them, provided for them, taught them, and conversed with them. And now, He's asking them to share their location with Him? This continues to happen though as so many Christians, formed by a good God, somehow find themselves depressed, addicted, divorced, carrying ungodly labels, and so much more. How did we get there? How did we go from being known by Him before we were in our mother's womb to now needing to share our location with Him?

At the end of the day, even though it's easy to mock Adam and Eve (and the rest of the Bible characters for that matter), we are no different than them. The only difference between us and the people referenced in Scripture is technology!

As hindsight is 20/20, it's very natural to assume we would do better if we were put in any of these situations. It's easy to think we would get God involved if we were talking to a serpent. Or maybe you find yourself on the other end of the spectrum. Maybe you look at the good these flawed people did and have a hard time identifying with it. We can often over-glorify and dehumanize the people referenced in Scripture. We read the stories of the heroes of our faith and envision them with a demigod glow. Maybe you've watered down their stories, their hardships, and their pain, forgetting that they were real people and not vegetables (no disrespect to VeggieTales). No one's life summed up on paper could possibly capture the true humanity that every moment entailed.

WE ALL FAIL TO REMEMBER THAT WE *ARE* EVE IN THE MIDDLE OF A DAILY CONVERSATION WITH A SERPENT.

Both sides fail to realize the very real psychological and spiritual battle that every Christian trying to honor God will face. We all fail to remember that we *are* Eve in the middle of a daily conversation with a serpent. We are all tempted to build a calf, to bow before man, to laugh, to doubt, to deny Christ, and so much more. The Christian life will not reflect the life of one of the Bible stories, rather a collection of all of them. This book will look at this clickbait battle, the clickbait dialogue we're all having with that serpent, and dive into how we can live the lives that God has made available to us!

Let's start by actually defining "clickbait". According to Merriam-Webster, "clickbait" is defined as "something (such as a headline) designed to make readers want to click on a hyperlink **especially** when the link leads to content of dubious value or interest."

I've highlighted the word "especially," as it leads us to believe the nature of the content is what makes it clickbait, not just the invitation itself. To get the full picture of this definition, we should also note that "dubious" means "not to be relied on; suspect." A quick reverse engineering of this definition would find that the content is suspect and shouldn't be relied on, so the content creator has to bait you to get what they ultimately want.

When we talk about clickbait in this book, we must understand the full weight of clickbait's dubious nature. Whenever your enemy hurls accusations in your direction, you can be sure his information is not to be relied on. It's suspect!

I'm sure every single person referenced in Scripture would have loved if Mirriam-Webster had existed back in their day. I'm sure they would have loved to know that the enemy's accusations were dubious and not to be relied on. I'm sure Eve wished she had known; I'm sure everyone wishes Eve had known! By taking the enemy's bait, Adam and Eve's sin paved a way for the struggle that each Bible character faced.

Eve was wandering around the garden, mindlessly strolling along, when the serpent baited her with a simple promise: "There's value on the other side of eating this fruit." She hesitated at first but ended up taking the bait, and what followed was more unsatisfying than anything on our Popular page.

Eve fell prey to clickbait. The enemy baited her into dialogue, and she took the bait. Eve's dialogue ended with them having to work much harder than God intended just to survive. It made bringing something new into the world very painful, and it brought shame upon them in an instant. Now that sin had entered the world, the battle with the enemy's clickbait was a battle we would all have to manage. And it was all because she took the bait.

We've all asked our own questions about the first woman's exchange with the tricky serpent. How could she have fallen for that? How did the serpent get into the perfect garden? Why didn't she just turn around and get God involved? Why didn't she just call God over and let Him deal with the serpent's questions?

Before we answer any of these questions, let's take a look at the actual story:

> *[1] Now the serpent was more crafty than any other beast of the field that the Lord God had made. He said to the woman, "Did God actually say, 'You shall not eat of any tree in the garden'?" [2] And the woman said to the serpent, "We may eat of the fruit of the trees in the garden, [3] but God said, 'You shall not eat of the fruit of the tree that is in the midst of the garden, neither shall you touch it, lest you die.'" [4] But the serpent said to the woman, "You will not surely die. [5] For God knows that when you eat of it your eyes will be opened, and you will be like God, knowing good and evil." [6] So when the woman saw that the tree was good for food, and that it was a delight to the eyes, and that the tree was to be desired to make one wise, she took of its fruit and ate, and she also gave some to her husband who was with her, and he ate. [7] Then the eyes of both were opened, and they knew that they were naked. And they sewed fig leaves together and made themselves loincloths. Genesis 3:1-7*

Every time I read this passage, I'm shocked at how much actually took place in seven simple verses. Seven short lines discuss the very first time one of us struggled with the enemy's clickbait, and it explains why the rest of us continue to struggle every day. This passage also gives us some very real insight into who our enemy is, and the tactics he likes to use. Three major things should stand out to us as we reread this passage:

Firstly, Eve didn't realize she was stepping into battle. Eve doesn't seem like someone who knew someone was coming against her! And who could blame her? Ephesians 6:12 says:

> *For we do not wrestle against flesh and blood, but against the rulers, against the authorities, against the cosmic powers over this present darkness, against the spiritual forces of evil in the heavenly places.*

This shows us our battle against clickbait is not an obvious one, as Eve's was not an obvious one either. It's not a war we wage in the flesh. I know that sounds so "duh," but do you realize that 99.99 percent of everything else we do is done in the flesh? We sleep, eat, and workout to take care of our flesh. We interact with people with our flesh. Our flesh is our only mode of transportation! It's hard to know when we are waging war in our flesh and when we are waging war in the spirit. The war for our minds is not an obvious one!

Secondly, did you notice the lack of introduction in this passage? I'm not sure Eve ever realized who she was speaking to, just like you and I have a hard time distinguishing where certain thoughts are even coming from. To be completely fair to Eve, it's not like the serpent introduced himself as her enemy. The devil wouldn't be much of a devil if he showed up to the battlefield and introduced himself. He can't have @YourEnemy as his social media handle or "seeking to steal, kill, and destroy" in his bio. He wouldn't be able to succeed in convincing Eve without masking the source of his clickbait.

Thirdly, I'm intrigued by what the serpent *didn't* say. A close look at what he did or did not say reveals a significant truth about his tactics. He didn't downright threaten her. He didn't proclaim to be higher than God. He simply intrigued her by questioning God's truth, and ultimately he got her to question God Himself by hurling a poorly defined insult at her.

The serpent's words to Eve were an accusation. To say "you will surely not die" is to imply she wasn't *really* living. But he didn't actually say that; he simply implied it. His tactic wasn't a knockout punch but a seemingly nonthreatening cut at what God had said.

MANAGING CLICKBAIT

The enemy ultimately wanted Eve's attention, and he got it. Christians are still in this battle today as the serpent is still trying to win over our attention. And he's not simply trying to tempt us into sin, but he's actively inviting us into mindsets and belief systems that imply we could never have all that God has made available to us.

"

THE WAR FOR OUR MINDS IS
NOT AN OBVIOUS ONE!

"

But he doesn't have to win; we can manage this fight! We can let God fight this battle for us. We can think thoughts that line up with God's truth and allow those thoughts to lead our lives into everything God has for His people.

The rest of this book will help you manage and win the war for your attention, starting with identifying the clickbait tactics the enemy will use on a daily basis. There are five subgroups of clickbait that each one of us has unwittingly allowed into the normalcy of our lives:

1. The Clickbait of Offense

No one ever gets offended on purpose. We don't consciously try to get hurt by something someone says or does. But our enemy will always use our tendency to take things personally against us in order to isolate us. If every good and perfect gift comes from God, and God is a relational God, then our enemy will always work to isolate the children of such a God. Isolation leads to desecration in the life of a Christian. Lucky for us, unless the volume is too loud, words seemingly only hurt when you let them.

2. The Clickbait of Reminiscing

It may seem normal to spend some time looking back, and nostalgia is a pretty normal part of our lives. But reminiscing can be dangerous too. Christ always calls us forward, so why would we spend any time looking back? God's call to acknowledge the new things He was doing started with a call to remember not the former things (Isaiah 43:19).

3. The Clickbait of Self-Diagnosis

We are all trying to figure out what may be wrong with us in hopes of getting ahead of it. That leads us to analyze our current reality, compare it unfairly to what we assume other people's reality is, and then diagnose our problem. Luckily you aren't an expert in *everything*. And that's exactly what you'd have to be to correctly self-diagnose—an expert in literally everything. God, the actual expert in everything, has already laid out our diagnosis!

4. The Clickbait of "Maybe"

I believe some people have unknowingly trademarked the word "maybe," even though it can be an antonym for faith. Peter didn't say, "Humble yourselves under the mighty hand of God and *maybe* God will exalt you" (1 Peter 5:6). James doesn't say, "God will exalt you! Well, *maybe*" (James 4:10). If we enter into the dialogue of "maybe," we won't make it out. "Maybe" is the true bottomless pit, as it can't be proven or disproven. "Maybe" gets us coming back into dialogue again and again, never coming to grips with the unknown future and the role faith plays in it. But we can have certainty in an uncertain world, and we can eradicate this horrible word from our vocabulary.

5. The Clickbait of Self-Pity

Helen Keller said, "Self-pity is our worst enemy, and if we yield to it, we can never do anything wise in this world." Every Christian and non-Christian alike fights the ever-present, nagging battle against feeling sorry for ourselves. No one ever won anything by feeling sorry for themselves! But a lot has been lost on the battlefield of self-pity. If our life moves in the direction of our strongest thoughts, then I can't imagine where someone's life ends up when they continue to feel sorry for themselves.

I know what you're thinking…most of these seem not only harmless but normal and purposeful in our lives. Many of us have even had authority figures look us right in the eye and tell us that one of these, if not all, are normal. And they're right! If we're defining "normal" by "a man's everyday experience," then yes, they are completely normal. But if we choose to define "normal" as "the things God has made available for His people," then no, they couldn't be farther from normal. Just because something happens frequently doesn't make it normal!

Our enemy uses these different, seemingly harmless clickbait techniques to divert your attention away from God's promises for your life. They get your mind in both yesterday and tomorrow, making it impossible for you to be where your feet are today. They get you talking to the serpent, who *will* talk back.

But we have hope today. Why? Because, in the wise words of my father, "if the enemy is talking, he's lying!"

CHAPTER 2

WHY CLICKBAIT?

Back in 2007, my dad suffered a massive widowmaker heart attack. Only five percent of the victims of the widowmaker survive, hence its name—and we're blessed to say my dad is in that five percent! God truly spared him and us all. But for a long time, I wrestled with why my dad would have had a heart attack at forty-six years old. There was clickbait coming at me from all sides. I wondered if it would happen again randomly or if something similar, or perhaps worse, would happen to me. I'll never forget the time I was driving a friend to the airport and my dad wouldn't answer his phone after a few calls. Horrible thoughts immediately came pouring in about what could have happened to him.

After years of the post-traumatic stress of such a life-altering event, we had to come to grips with something: this single event was not because of one other event. This horrible situation did not have one simple cause or one simple solution. I've heard rockstars say that they aren't an overnight success, rather that they worked hard for twenty years to become an overnight success. In the same way, this tragedy didn't surface overnight. It was all the little choices to have fast food over the years. It wasn't one event but thousands and thousands of small events.

As we dive into the battle for our attention against clickbait, it is important to understand our enemy isn't looking for a knockout blow. No, he likes the "death by a thousand cuts" approach much more. It's not about taking you out today; it's about using today to take you out tomorrow. It's about cutting you today, and later today, and tomorrow, and the next day. We know from Scripture that this battle is not against flesh and blood, which again means we won't be able to see it, feel it, or touch it. It's a spiritual battle. It's not a war we wage in our flesh, rather a war our flesh wages with our spirit.

How does the enemy cut you? What is his blade of choice? His weapons are the countless voices that come at us twenty-four hours a day, seven days a week, fifty-two weeks a year. His weapon is the constant barrage of thoughts and voices coming at us from each and every direction imaginable. Each thought, each voice, isn't a knockout blow by any means, but they add up. Like a bad diet, a bad thought life clogs the arteries of your soul without any sign of real danger until it's too late.

Christians have to sift through more thoughts and voices today than ever before because there's a whole lot of noise in our lives. We live in a day and age where we have access to too many people, and we've become overwhelmed with their opinions. It's hard to know who's for you and who's against you, who's trying to help you and who has an agenda. With all the social media influencers, Instagram pastors, blogs, and everything else in this overly connected world, it's increasingly more difficult to sift through it all and hear God's voice.

MANY HARD GAMES

There's a store near our house that I just can't go to anymore. Ever since I was a kid, I knew the success of my life would depend on avoiding this store at all costs. They didn't sell anything gross; quite the contrary actually. They sold cologne! But it was more like a market; there were tons of brands with booths manned by salesmen determined to sell their exotic fragrances. They were lined up on this long hallway, connecting one side of the mall to the other, and their sales technique was clear: spray first, talk later. I liked stores on both sides, so sometimes I knew I was going to have to man up and take the long walk through the cologne-infused mist the salesmen would douse me in.

I'm not exaggerating. It would've been easier to play paintball in an open field than to go into that store without getting sprayed. One after the other, they would bombard every customer with their cologne hoping to get their attention. You couldn't even get a good sense of what

LIKE A BAD DIET, A BAD THOUGHT LIFE CLOGS THE ARTERIES OF YOUR SOUL WITHOUT ANY SIGN OF REAL DANGER UNTIL IT'S TOO LATE.

any of them smelled like, you'd just carry around a mix of 30 different colognes all day.

This is the picture I get whenever I think about our thought life on a normal day. The famous saying says, "The barking dog gets fed first." Our mind is full of 30 different barking dogs all wanting to get fed. We have our jobs, countless relationships, dreams, our health, bills, responsibilities, chores, and much more. This wouldn't be so bad in a vacuum, but each is like a game: there is an outcome that will be judged. There will be a winner on one side and a loser on the other. You'll have winning seasons and losing seasons in each of these areas.

The outcomes depend on the rules and strategies, which require certain knowledge in order to win. In many of them, it involves teammates that you can't control. Anyone playing a game must be mindful of each rule and boundary at all times while applying the chosen strategy and remembering the quirks and tendencies of each teammate. And successfully balancing all of this still doesn't guarantee victory!

To make matters worse, there is constant criticism of every step and decision. The coaches, teammates, and fans are all instantaneously responding to each move and choice you make in real time. And then you have to include your own snap judgment for each action as well, expecting more from everyone around you but also expecting more from yourself.

This, and even more, is at play in each of our friendships, our career choices, our health, and so much more. Like a crowd of a hundred thousand raving fans, our mind is judging every move we make in every game we play. We're all just trying our best to win, as we're playing a hundred games at once. I don't want this truth to make you feel sorry for yourself (as we will soon dive into how devoid of value self-pity really is shortly). But we all have a lot more going on than we may realize, and we must be aware we have an enemy who will take advantage of all that to cut our legs out from underneath us every chance he gets.

We've already listed a few of those games like our career, friends, family members, personal projects, athletic pursuits, and artistic endeavors. Now add a spiritual battle between our flesh and God's Spirit living on the inside of us. Add putting our eternal fate in a God we cannot see.

Add bad weather, traffic, and a hundred different people with a hundred different emotions, desires, and shortcomings to juggle.

Yeah, there's a lot of mental cologne swirling around. Let's take a second to celebrate you getting this far. I genuinely believe you should take a moment to acknowledge how much you've fought through, how much you carry, and just how far you've come through it all!

At the same time, we all have to realize just how many voices we have to sift through every day. We have to know that there are some voices trying to help us, others saying they're trying to help us but they're only trying to help themselves, and some genuinely trying to hurt us. Just like Eve, the outcome of our lives will depend on the voices that we listen to.

I believe all these voices can be summed into four major categories, and differentiating between the four will help significantly as we battle through this war with clickbait. But before we jump into the list, we must acknowledge this simple truth—you aren't responsible for all of the voices out there; you're only responsible for the ones you listen to. We aren't responsible for all of the food around the table, just the food that we consume.

RIGHT VOICES, RIGHT CHOICES

In 2021, our pastor said we were going to focus on wisdom as a church. So he challenged us to read the book of Proverbs every single month for the year. We'd read whatever chapter corresponded with the day. It took a few months, but eventually the ninth became my favorite day of the month! Read the first few verses, and you'll quickly see why.

> *Wisdom has built her house; she has hewn her seven pillars. [2] She has slaughtered her beasts; she has mixed her wine; she has also set her table. [3] She has sent out her young women to call from the highest places in the town, "Whoever is simple, let him turn in here!"*
> *Proverbs 9:1–4a*

Lady Wisdom sounds like a good social media follow! She could probably do a TEDx talk on slaying beasts, the real estate market, winemaking, or how to feast. Wisdom wouldn't have to buy fake followers. But this isn't why Proverbs 9 became my favorite. Let's look at the rest of that chapter:

> *The woman Folly is loud; she is seductive and knows nothing.* [14] *She sits at the door of her house; she takes a seat on the highest places of the town,* [15] *calling to those who pass by, who are going straight on their way,* [16] *"Whoever is simple, let him turn in here!" Proverbs 9:13–16a*

A second character, Lady Folly, is introduced. She doesn't sound like as good a hang. She's always late on trends, stealing content from everyone else and just cropping out the branding. She doesn't have much in common with our new best friend, Lady Wisdom.

But they do have one thing in common; according to this passage they are sitting in the same seats, singing the same song. Both passages elaborate on what they're actually saying, and I encourage you to take a deeper look into it! But this chapter became my favorite because it explains why juggling all the different games of life is so hard; wisdom and folly can be hard to distinguish at first. It's like those famous commercials with the sign flippers; folly may have some appealing tricks, but you can't actually read the sign.

The differences between what is wise and what is foolish is not black and white, it's very gray. Proverbs doesn't shy away from this either: "There is a way that seems right to a man, but its end is the way to death" (Proverbs 14:12). There is a way in life, in relationships, in your career, and in your thinking in general that really seems like the right way; but it actually leads to your destruction.

Remember Lot? He listened to the angel and didn't look back, and the destruction behind him didn't overtake him. But his wife listened to a different voice and was turned into a salt shaker. The Israelites and even some Egyptians listened to Moses and painted the blood of the lamb over the door posts, and the death angel passed over their homes on one of the deadliest nights in their history. Shadrach, Meshach, and Abednego chose not to listen to the voices of that day and watched as God was in the fire with them. Even Jesus had to choose the written Word of God over the voice He was hearing in the desert. You aren't responsible for all of the voices coming at you; you're only responsible for the ones you listen to!

It's important to distinguish the differences between these voices and equally important to know what to do with them. Giving false authority to certain voices can, like for Adam and Eve, create an inner hell in the midst of paradise. Once we create hell on the inside, it's not too long until we start to see hell on the outside. Let's differentiate among all the different voices begging for our attention! I believe they can be summed up into four main voices:

1. The voice that created the world (God's voice)
2. The loudest voice (people's voices)
3. The voice that creates your world (your voice)
4. The invisible voice (the voice in your head)

ONCE WE CREATE HELL ON THE INSIDE, IT'S NOT TOO LONG UNTIL WE START TO SEE HELL ON THE OUTSIDE.

The first voice was the voice that said, "Let there be light!" It's the same voice that said, "Let there be YOU." This voice, the voice of our God, creates. It created the air we breathe, the lungs that take in that air, and the internal process that uses that air to keep us alive. It's the same voice that called you, named you, and identified you as His own.

The second voice is the voice of other people. This voice can be the loudest. I've always been baffled by a common phrase uttered by the world's most successful athletes, especially when a microphone is shoved in their face in their finest moments: "They all said I couldn't do it!" Here they've clearly proved "them" wrong, whoever they are; and yet their voice is still ringing in their ears. That's because this voice weighs the most, or at least we think it does. This is the voice that has fueled the greatest among us to their highest heights and thrown each of us to our lowest lows. Like Ricky Bobby, we all hear our dad screaming, "If you ain't first, you're last!"

This voice can break our bones more than any stick or stone, as Proverbs 17:22 (NIV) says: "A cheerful heart is good medicine, but a crushed spirit dries up the bones." But, this voice only weighs as much as we allow it.

The third voice, your voice, is the voice that creates your world. You may be thinking, "Wouldn't that be God's voice?" Yes, God's voice has created the world. But I've watched too many people create a life very different than the one God made available to them. That's because the voice that creates our world is our *own* voice. This voice models God's voice, as we were made in His image.

Our voice seems to go in tandem with our heart, our innermost being; out of the abundance of the heart, the mouth speaks (Matthew 12:24). This voice has crazy, sneaky power. This voice is significantly more powerful than people's voices. "They" may say you can't, but that's not anywhere near as stifling as when *you* say you can't. This voice has created the current predicament you find yourself in way more than any of us would like to admit.

The fourth and final voice, what I call the "invisible" voice, the voice in your head, is the one we're going to spend the most time on throughout this book. This voice is the most confusing. This voice sounds like God sometimes, like you at other times, and like a stranger at other times. This voice baffles the greatest among the philosophers and psychologists, as no one seems to know where this invisible voice comes from! This is that odd voice in your head.

This is the voice that says, "you'll never," before you've even tried. This voice says, "maybe you're just . . . ," when the Bible, your pastor, and your parents say the opposite. Like the moon, this voice doesn't have its own source of light, but it still feels like it does. This voice is the only voice with a volume dial we can control. It has zero influence to create unless it's given that authority. This voice is insignificant and lifeless unless your voice echoes its worthless cries. We may not know where it comes from, but it's abundantly clear that this voice is the battleground for clickbait, and our enemy is really good at making his voice sound like our voice.

Distinguishing between these voices is vital in the life of a Christian. Thankfully the enemy doesn't know who he's messing with. After his conversation with Eve, the very next conversation the serpent found himself in was with God Himself. And this conversation was a monologue, not a dialogue (Genesis 3:14–15).

Have peace in knowing that God wants to fight this battle for you, that He is fighting it for you, and that He will win. Take heart in knowing you aren't the only one caught in a dialogue with the serpent. Be thankful today that we're all in this together! And remember, if he's talking, he's lying!

THERE IS NO TRUTH IN THEIR MOUTH

The enemy can't say anything that is true or even remotely in the direction of truth. He isn't truth, he doesn't know truth, and can't even point to truth. He stands on the opposite side of truth! King David understood this and the role that truth played in his own life. In Psalm 5:8–10, he says:

> *[8] Lead me, O Lord, in your righteousness because of my enemies; make your way straight before me. [9] For there is no truth in their mouth; their inmost self is destruction; their throat is an open grave; they flatter with their tongue. [10] Make them bear their guilt, O God; let them fall by their own counsels; because of the abundance of their transgressions cast them out, for they have rebelled against you.*

What a powerful statement! We should make shirts and iPhone backgrounds that say "There is no truth in the mouth of my enemy." As great as that is to hear, it's still very hard to fathom. The only reason we struggle at all is because some of what he says sounds true, right? If truth is a solid rock, then we'd never struggle if we could always tell what was true from what was false.

I'm not taking on the impossible task of clearly defining truth today, but David gives us some insight that can help us identify truth from the lies. After saying there is no truth in the mouth of his enemies, he says that his enemies have rebelled against God (Psalm 5:10). He's saying that his enemies aren't coming after him; rather they are opposing God Himself. They didn't gear up to fight a war against David but against God. That shows us that the serpent was coming against God, not simply trying to deceive Eve. Our enemy is not trying to become a wedge between God and His creation; instead he is standing on the opposing line of the battlefield.

“

Have peace in knowing that God wants to fight this battle for you, that He is fighting it for you, and that He will win.

This isn't simple semantics or profound imagery; this is recognizing the battle that's going on every minute of every day in the spiritual realm and our place in it. The implications of this truth are astounding, and we'll get into them throughout the remainder of this book. But for now, let's simply take the resounding battle lines that this truth has drawn.

We've recognized that we have an enemy that's opposing God, throwing anything at us to see what sticks. This enemy is luring us into dialogue using clickbait, trying to distract us and remove us from God's truth. We've identified his method: "death by a thousand cuts." We've learned that there isn't any room for truth in his mouth, and he's incapable of providing anything of any value to us.

As clear as that is on paper, it's still incredibly difficult to live out over the long haul. Just like my dad's heart attack wasn't caused overnight and didn't have a quick fix, climbing out of the hole of our enemy's clickbait will not be a one-time decision and will not be defeated once and for all. Just like we have to die to ourselves daily, we're going to have to fight this battle with clickbait daily.

Let's take a look at our first clickbait tactic, the clickbait of offense.

PART 2

CLICKBAIT

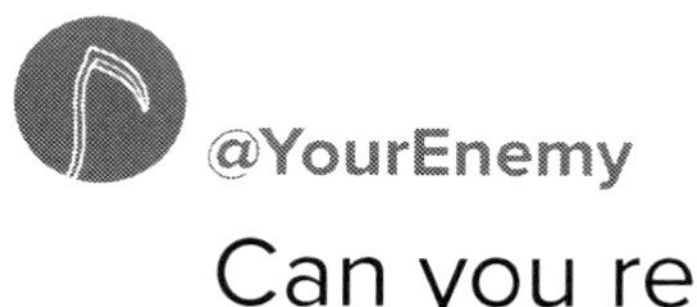
@YourEnemy
Can you really trust them?

CHAPTER 3

THE CLICKBAIT OF OFFENSE

We've all heard it before: if you *can* be offended, you *will* be. Good, hard-working Christians have believed this sentiment and aim to rise above offense, yet every one of us gets offended. No one does it on purpose! We don't consciously go into a conversation looking to get offended, but we watch people leave conversations offended every single day. We cut off friendships, leave churches, get divorced, and harbor hurt feelings against insanely large groups of people (most of which we don't even know) all because we have been offended.

There isn't one of us that is above the temptation to get offended. We all fall short of the glory of God, and we all fall short of our desire to rise above offense.

How does this happen? How do we all post such inspirational thoughts, give such great advice, and yet still manage to get offended? How does it get us when we know it's coming?

The people of the Bible struggled with the clickbait of offense. Why did Eve assume God was holding something back from her? Why did Rebekah favor Jacob over Esau, and why was it so easy for Jacob to follow through with her plan and rob from his brother? Why did the Israelites naturally believe God's plan was to kill them, and why did they think that so often?

Because it's easy to lose the still, small voice in the midst of the earthquake. It's easier to react to the heat from the fire than the warmth of His embrace.

Every Christian will struggle with the clickbait of offense, tempted to believe everyone is doing everything against them on purpose. While the enemy has deployed his "death by a thousand cuts" method, he hurls every thought imaginable at us to get us to believe the people we love are the ones doing the damage. The enemy knows we have a propensity to take things personally, so it's easy to bait us into believing our friends, our parents, our spouse, or our leaders are the ones cutting us down. Then we're baited to believe that all our pain would cease if that person would stop behaving that way.

Those who have given into the clickbait of offense sound like this:

- "They just have it out for me."
- "I've never really liked them, and they've never really liked me."
- "They just don't understand."
- "That's just how they are."

Whenever someone hurts you, the clickbait of offense makes you think the other person acted with you specifically in mind. It gets you to subconsciously believe that the other person has a dartboard with your face on it, and they devote their precious time devising ways to ruin your life. It convinces you that you are the main character of everyone's story, and the only emotions the supporting cast can feel are jealousy, resentment, and anger.

I'm sure reading that last statement was harsh, but that's truly what we do when we're offended. Look at the examples I listed about offense! They all create two parties: you and them. Somehow, in this moment, you believe you know more about their intentions than they do! You almost imagine them rehearsing their lines for tomorrow's performance.

But notice, in each of these examples and the countless more that exist, they all say more about you than the other person. You may believe they are obsessed with hurting you, but aren't you the one thinking about them even when they aren't around? You think they're rehearsing their lines, but aren't you rehearsing their rehearsal?

We subconsciously believe that we would enter into world peace if our friend would stop posting that way, if our pastor would stop talking about

“

Every Christian will struggle with the clickbait of offense, tempted to believe everyone is doing everything against them on purpose.

money, if our elders kept their noses out of our love life, and if our parents would just let us live. But even if that all happened, we'd soon realize that it wasn't the source of our pain at all. The clickbait of offense convinces us that people need to live and let live, when the only person who truly has the power to lock you up is staring at you in the mirror.

The clickbait of offense convinces you that you are not liked, that you are caged, that people are obstacles to your happiness, all because the enemy's voice has no power to create these things! He must co-opt your voice to create a relational hell. Whenever we give into offense, we are walking ourselves into a jail cell and closing the door, even though the door is unlocked.

ISO-VERT

I found myself binging nature shows for about three months while searching for something to relax with after work. They were the perfect before-bed shows: captivating enough to entertain, but not so interesting as to keep me from sleeping. I started to dream in David Attenborough's voice. It was pure bliss.

If you were to turn on any nature show right now (or after you're done with this chapter), you'd be quick to find an episode about predators vs. prey. Whenever a pride of lions or a few hunting dogs are ready to eat, they'll just run at the pack of gazelles or whatever their dinner of choice is. They come from all angles and sides, running aimlessly alongside or throughout the pack. But their seemingly random behavior is actually very tactical, as they work to isolate a single member of the pack. Once a single gazelle takes a wrong turn, each predator forgets the pack and sets their sights on the isolated prey. That gazelle is no match for them, running for as long as it can before giving up.

> OFFENDED PEOPLE BECOME ISOLATED PEOPLE.

I don't mean to be graphic, but this analogy explains why our enemy deploys the clickbait of offense. Offended people become isolated people.

Once you feel offended by someone at church, it's not long before you feel like that person has co-opted everyone else at church into their hatred of you. You walk into the lobby believing all eyes are on you and not in the way you want. You happen to miss a Sunday, and now you feel like they're all talking about how you missed service.

No one can deal with that type of treatment for too long, so naturally you decide you'll just watch online. Now there's no need to watch at any particular time, not to mention no one to serve. After a few weeks, you start watching on Sunday evening because it fits your schedule better. And after a month of Sunday night watch parties, there's no one checking in on you. Maybe they aren't checking in because they know you've cut them off, but all you can think is, "how could 'Christians' just forget me like this?" You start to remember everything you did for the church, and this is how they repay you?! Before long, you stop watching altogether. Now you have no Godly community. Welcome to hotel isolation!

Or let's say a parental figure or a leader in your life doesn't like the person you're with, romantically or a simple friend. Your love for this person, platonic or romantic, supersedes anything this leadership figure could say. You continue to hang out or date this person, deciding to keep all details of your relationship private. A barrier has now been set up in your heart, separating what you can share with them and what you can't. You now have two worlds: one with your parents or leaders and the other with this person.

But no one can live in two worlds for long, and you have to decide what world to fully live in. You either cut off the leaders pulling you forward toward your best self so you can be with the one you love, or you listen to those leaders and break your own heart, admitting they were right from the start. The latter is too painful, so you dive even deeper into the relationship. But now you're even more invested in this relationship because of everything you gave up for it, which means the relationship was just forced to change overnight. Now you're checked in to the Isolation Inn, where guests rarely check out.

It would have been easier to never entertain the world outside of your parents or leaders and believe God would bring someone who fits that world. It would be easier to take your lumps in the church lobby, leaving the rest to God! But the clickbait of offense gets in there and cuts you off from Godly relationships and ultimately your relationship with God.

When we talk about isolation, we're not talking about introversion. Introverts are simply people who like to recharge alone or in a small group. But isolation speaks of physical and emotional separation. Our enemy's goal isn't the loneliness part; it's the separation. His win isn't in the emotions you feel; it's in the lost opportunity of a God-centered community. Our enemy deploys the clickbait of offense to separate you from your pack. It's a good tactic too. It makes total sense! Look at what Scripture has to say about "the pack":

- "And let us not neglect our meeting together, as some people do, but encourage one another, especially now that the day of his return is drawing near." Hebrews 10:25 (NLT)
- "Without counsel plans fail, but with many advisers they succeed." Proverbs 15:22
- "For where two or three are gathered in my name, there am I among them." Matthew 18:20
- "This is the third time I am coming to you. Every charge must be established by the evidence of two or three witnesses." 2 Corinthians 13:1–2

It's abundantly clear that good things happen to those in the pack. According to Scripture, God is in the midst of the pack. Wisdom and even clear judgment are in the midst of the pack. Of course any enemy worth his salt would try and separate us from all the blessings of a God-centered pack!

The goal of the clickbait of offense is to isolate and separate us, and there are dire results if it succeeds. Like pride before a fall, isolation comes before the complete destruction of one's faith.

SHADOWS

Enemies are like shadows; we don't have to create them ourselves. They just exist. If you just live your life normally, there's bound to be a few enemies along the way. We didn't do anything personally to deserve the devil. No, we have an enemy courtesy of Adam and Eve's mistake.

And yet, even with natural-born enemies, so many of us continue to go around creating more. I don't mean creating a rival, like the Joker to our Batman. I'm talking about our very real ability to demonize those who don't see things like we do, say things like we do, or believe like we do. We literally create demons out of ordinary people who have a different perspective.

This is what the clickbait of offense does: offense creates enemies out of people that would ordinarily add value to your life.

Let me demonstrate this process using yet another *The Office* reference. There seems to be two types of people in this world: the Angelo Grottis and the Michael Scotts. Angelo Grotti is the fake mobster/actual insurance rep from *The Office* who's most known for his famous line, "If it is not on the side, I send it back." We all know an Angelo Grotti. These are the people who cause the rest of us to avoid looking the waiter in the eye after they send back a perfectly good meal. They are the ones that insist on getting a new burger because their mind can't fathom scraping the mayonnaise off. Grottis send back cheese fries because of the scallions.

The rest of us find more in common with Michael Scott. We just deal with whatever is brought to us. Is it what we ordered? Nope. But the thought of what our waiter may do with our new plate of food is far scarier than a few scallions. We can't fathom living with ourselves if a random waiter has a less-than-satisfactory opinion of us. You can spot a Michael Scott in any restaurant; they're the ones losing their appetite as Grotti gets into it with a waiter.

My grandma is a Scott. She taught me to be a Scott. I hated eggs when I was nine years old, but she wouldn't let me go play with my cousins until I finished eating them. They finished theirs, and now I needed to finish mine. I had to deal with what was in front of me.

My grandfather was a Grotti through and through. This man sent back enough soup to fill a rather large lake, all because it didn't (I repeat, *did not*) burn his lips on his first bite. My grandfather Alessi had sent back *something* he ordered on at least 80 percent of the meals we've shared together, and that's no exaggeration. Whenever we would go to a restaurant with

OFFENSE CREATES ENEMIES OUT OF PEOPLE THAT WOULD ORDINARILY ADD VALUE TO YOUR LIFE.

him, we all brought our hard hats; we just knew it was going to hit the fan at some point. We weren't even bothered by it anymore!

Whenever we are offended, like a Grotti, we are tempted to shift the burden of responsibility of fixing it to the person who's wronged us. The voice in our head says things like, "This isn't what I want, so they should fix it." This dialogue erupts in our head without our permission, simultaneously discussing how much we've done for that person and how we would hypothetically have handled that situation better than they did.

To be perfectly honest, this is entirely justifiable behavior. Your anger is justified. Your pain is justified. Ephesians 4:26 even tells us we can be angry! Being hurt isn't wrong. This inner dialogue has not crossed over into sinful territory yet.

But if the anger turns into creating an enemy out of this person, we have now sinned. We have chosen to label this person's actions as an offense that needs forgiveness. The very act of labeling their action an offense that needs forgiving makes us someone harboring unforgiveness. We wouldn't need to forgive them if we hadn't started to harbor unforgiveness. But it's too late for that; we've already assumed their actions were personal and thus created a good guy and a bad guy, a victor and a victim.

We've stepped out of Christ's "more than a conqueror" spirit and into a victim mentality. We have labeled this person unworthy of forgiveness, simultaneously labeling us as someone worthy of it. This isn't the cause, it's the effect. It's the equal and opposite reaction to every action. It's the shadow that is automatically created wherever there is light.

We don't do these things consciously, but it all happens instantaneously. It's far easier to never label the person's actions as an offense that needs forgiving. It's far easier to let it fall like water off a duck's back. It's far easier to shift from the victim to the victor and aim to bring life rather than your own sword to these situations.

Whenever someone hurts you, I want you to think: that's a *them* problem. It's a problem with them. Let them deal with it. No, I'm not saying send it back like Grotti and think only they could solve it. Not at all. I'm saying you have to refuse to become part of the problem. If the problem started with them, let it end with you. Try and become part of the solution! Sit there and deal with it.

However, I'm also not saying to accept unfair treatment. I'm not saying we should submit ourselves to abuse. This is not a call to accept everything; it's a call to accept the responsibility of creating the lives God has made available to us. No one can rob of us of that, even if they try. As we pursue the life God has made available to us, we should deal with our problems head-on. If it's in front of us, we should deal with it. If someone has hurt us, we should pursue them to patch things up.

IF THE PROBLEM STARTED WITH THEM, LET IT END WITH YOU.

PATCHING THINGS UP

Can you imagine sitting in a prison for a crime you did not commit, far from home and any family, because your family disowned you and left you to indecent people? Then can you imagine getting out of that prison and working your way up to running Amazon?

That's basically a modern-day version of Joseph's story in Genesis. Joseph is sold into slavery by his brothers, accused of a crime he did not commit, thrown into prison, then released and rises through the ranks to become the second-in-command of the entire land! If anyone had a reason to get offended, it was Joseph. There's no way to paint what his brothers did as anything other than complete and total hatred and jealousy. And yet the Lord was with Joseph (Genesis 39:2).

The story gets weird, though, as one day they end up approaching Joseph in their biggest moment of need. They drove the knife even deeper by completely failing to recognize him and by being ridiculously protective of their new youngest brother who had replaced Joseph as their father's favorite. Talk about pain.

The story is too long to sum up here, and I encourage you to take a look at it in Genesis 37–50. You'll see Joesph do some weird stuff. He accuses them of trying to spy on the land and throws them into prison for three days (Genesis 42:6–17). He ties up one of his brothers in front of the rest (Genesis 42:24). He breaks down crying numerous times (Genesis 42:24, 43:30). He tests them in some pretty odd ways too! I won't lie: the whole story is hard to follow.

But what we find is this: Joseph was strong in the pit, he was strong in slavery, he was strong in prison, and he was strong in the palace. But he was an emotional mess when his brothers came to patch things up. On multiple occasions, Joseph is a wreck internally even though he's thrived in Egypt.

You may be thinking, this is proof that isolation does help! He was fine as long as they weren't around. But I say it proves the opposite. Apparently, decades of being isolated from his family didn't fix anything. Even rising to the highest heights of fame and success didn't solve his problems. Being in a position of power to pay back his brothers for the hurt they caused him didn't make him feel any better either.

Instead, I think Joseph learned that isolation doesn't fix a thing. Isolation isn't of God, which means it is incapable of providing any life for you. The clickbait of offense uses isolation to turn us into our own worst enemy. So let's kick offense to the curb, aim to deal with whatever offense we're holding onto, and hold onto the pack instead!

THE FINE PRINT

KNOW: The enemy's main goal is isolation.

LOOK OUT FOR: The main character syndrome. You're great! But...

REMEMBER: Good things happen in the pack! And isolation never fixes anything.

DO: Lean into Godly community, even if it hurts! Isolation hurts more.

Can tomorrow
really be better
than today?

CHAPTER 4

THE CLICKBAIT OF REMINISCING

I'll never forget the day my dad finally gave in. He looked at me and said the words, "Come on, let's go." These four simple words were music to my ears. My life had just changed. I knew right then and there that I had arrived. I knew my classmates would have to treat me with more respect at school on Monday. They wouldn't be looking at the Chris Alessi of old; they would be looking at the new Chris Alessi, proud owner of a motorized scooter.

When we got to the store, I raced to the scooters with the flames and the racing stripes. This was when my dad pulled rank and offered a compromise: if I was going to get the scooter, it would have to be bright enough to be seen in the dark. So we left the racing stripes, and my dad picked the one he felt matched our compromise. He picked the absolute brightest yellow motorized scooter on the market. NASA would be able to see me riding around our neighborhood at night.

Before we left the store, the owner told me to test drive it around the parking lot. I slowly drove it all around the lot, testing the limits of my new bright yellow scooter. I hesitantly took every speed bump, every turn, and every crack in the pavement; and that yellow scooter held its own.

As I was coming to the far side of the parking lot my dad told me to speed up a bit, so I pushed down on the accelerator and sped up. I did everything I had just done, just a little faster. He told me to speed up again, and so I was a good son and did as I was told. But now each turn, each bump, was a little scarier than the first two times around. As I saw the speed bump approaching, I slowed down. My dad, knowing I was only going about ten miles an hour, told me to speed up again. I declined. He told me again, and I declined again. Right as he went to encourage me a third time, I turned to tell him to stop, and I lost control.

I didn't hit anything. I wasn't hit by anything. I just lost control!

I wasn't too hurt, as I said, I was only going around seven to ten miles an hour, but I learned a very valuable lesson that day. This lesson stayed with me when my dad taught me to ride a motorcycle, and when we drove four-wheelers around our family farm. This lesson has aided me whenever we take the wave runners out with some friends, or the time we rode snowmobiles through Yellowstone National Park in below-zero-degree weather.

The lesson is this, it's all about eye placement.

I didn't lose control because I was going too fast. The terrain didn't magically become any harder to manage. I lost control because I took my eyes off of the road. I simply looked in the wrong direction.

When you and I direct our eyes in the wrong direction—anywhere other than directly before us—we actually "lose" control. We freely give it up. Which explains why the enemy is throwing so much clickbait at us: to get our eyes off of where we're going and give up the reins.

I'm not talking about looking to God and giving Him control; we should obviously do that. God always has been and always will be in control. But just like an iceberg is 90 percent below the surface and 10 percent above it, there's a portion of control that God has given to us. And when we take our eyes off of where we're going, we give up that portion of control.

If you were to look at the serpent's opening statement to Eve, you'll see he was addressing the past. His first line was, "Did God really say you shall not eat of any tree in the garden?" Now, I'm not trying to put something into the Bible that isn't there! But, his first line was addressing something God said yesterday. It was turning her eyes to the past. To make matters worse, it wasn't even what God had said! But it didn't matter, they were already in dialogue. She had taken her eyes off of her work, off of what

God had put them in the garden to do, and she found herself knee deep in a dialogue that would change her life forever.

This is where the danger of reminiscing comes in. Like Eve mindlessly taking a stroll in the park, our enemy lifts up seemingly harmless talking points to get us to engage. It has to start out harmlessly because we clearly wouldn't engage unless we had a shot at beating him. We engage with this seemingly harmless activity of reminiscing, but that slowly turns into comparing today to yesterday. We direct your eyes to a younger self, a simpler self, and believe those days were better. We may be right! But that thought isn't the problem. The problem comes when we start comparing, and eventually we think we can win if we go backward instead of forward.

Reminiscing and nostalgia are sweet and mostly harmless activities but only if they lead to a place where we realize just how far God has taken us. If they take us to any other conclusion, we have taken the clickbait of reminiscing.

The clickbait of reminiscing sounds like this:

- "I used to be happier."
- "I didn't use to have this problem."
- "They used to treat me better."
- "I used to hear God so clearly."
- "Life used to be simpler."

None of these thoughts are a knockout punch by any stretch of the imagination. But again, our enemy has taken the "death by a thousand cuts" approach. A Christian whose eyes are placed anywhere but in front of them is a distracted Christian.

THE GOOD OLD DAYS...ISH

Remember the good old days? Most of us would probably say yes. We can all look back to a simpler time with less burden and battle. We all drive by our old school, house, church, job, etc. and feel overwhelmed with nostalgia. We remember those days with a ray of sunshine surrounding

A Christian whose eyes are placed anywhere but in front of them is a distracted Christian.

each memory. We've all told someone younger than us to enjoy where they're at, because it doesn't last!

I recently took my wife, Richelle, on a nostalgic trip back to my "good old days" stomping grounds. I showed her my childhood home, my high school, and our first church building. I went to the back behind the church to the old concrete lot. We would play football and have just about every youth and kids ministry event back there, and we even set up a basketball hoop with a three-point line and everything. Most of my memories as a kid came from that old concrete lot behind the church.

As I showed my wife all of this, I longed to experience those days again. I started to get emotional as I shared story after story with her. They were my glory days! But then I started to realize how much smaller it was than I had remembered. And then I realized our court was sandwiched between two dumpsters. I never thought about it too hard as a kid, but I suddenly remembered how many times we'd fight over whether the dumpsters were out of bounds or not. It wasn't long before I admitted that the good old days seemed a lot better in my head!

I'm going to take a wild guess and say the same is true for you. With a clear head, we'd all admit life gets far better as it goes along. Yet many of us still internally struggle with believing the past was better than it actually was.

Reminiscing is mostly harmless, as nostalgia can create truly sweet moments among long-term friends. Because of this, you're probably having an imaginary debate with me and this chapter about the accuracy of your thought. You're thinking yesterday was *genuinely* better! But this chapter is not here to debate the accuracy of these thoughts, but rather the implications that come if we consider these thoughts accurate.

We tend to lose hope when we feel we should go back to the way things were. We trip over our feet and land square on our face, unable to make any progress. That's why King Solomon warns us against giving into the clickbait of reminiscing. He says, "Say not, 'Why were the former days better than these?' For it is not from wisdom that you ask this" (Ecclesiastes 7:10).

He doesn't say it's a sin or even imply that it will kill you. The wisest man to ever live simply says reminiscing is unwise. Just like feeding the ducks isn't the brightest idea! At first, there's nothing wrong with the simple, sweet gesture—until they keep coming back. Most of the time, they come back believing yesterday's gesture is today's birthright.

Simply put, Solomon says it's unwise to think about yesterday being better than today. Because let's be honest, was it *that* much better? Are you 100 percent certain the younger you was a better you? Maybe the younger you was more agile, but does that mean better? Are you sure the way people treat you now is undoubtedly worse than before? Was your faith walk actually *better* yesterday than today?

A GAME NOT WORTH PLAYING

It's our inability to stop our thoughts at simple nostalgia that makes reminiscing unwise. Whenever we reminisce, it's not long before we start to compare; and comparison is a killer of joy. It's a game not worth playing!

When we compare, we tend to pick one avenue of our lives, one of the many hard games we referenced in chapter 2. We then make a decision as to whether we believe that one avenue was better yesterday. Then we make the dangerous and incorrect assumption that every avenue used to be better too.

Let's look at a Biblical example. In Numbers 14:1–4, the Israelites make a ridiculous claim that slavery in Egypt was better than wandering around in the desert. Even more ridiculous than the claim itself is how much they meant what they said! But was slavery in Egypt really better than taking the journey to the Promised Land? Maybe one night in the desert was worse than one night in their Egyptian homes, but did that mean slavery was better than freedom?

Of course not. And yet the Israelites convinced themselves that their time in Egypt was better. Even after the ten plagues. Even after crossing the Red Sea. Even while God led them with smoke and fire.

But can we blame them? We make silly comparisons like this all the time!

We compare our current job to our last job, saying our boss treated us better at the last job. Maybe looking at the single avenue of how one person treated you puts a win in the old job column, but that's forgetting the other avenues at play. It's forgetting that you got promoted at your current job. It was before you proved you could handle more than your old job. It was before your boss decided you could be trusted with the real them, and not the politician-like version of themselves that has to perform around people that don't know their hearts yet.

Yes, maybe being single did give you more "you" time. But more "you" time also came without a person to share all your other time with. It also meant sleeping alone, living alone, or operating outside of God's principles if you didn't do those things alone while single.

Yes, maybe it was easier to be happy back in college, but that was a more ignorant version of you! Ignorance is bliss, right? No.

It wasn't any better back then, it was just easier. And every sport, board game or video game has taught us that more reward comes with greater difficulty.

I'm not saying there aren't any outliers. There are some bosses that you shouldn't work for. There are people you shouldn't do life with. There are mistakes that ruin a large chunk of our lives. We all have to make our health a more active priority with each passing day, but even in these cases, nothing gets better by looking backward.

WIKIPEDIA BRAIN

Not only is reminiscing dangerous, but it's also false. We don't remember yesterday as clearly as we think we do! Like my old youth group parking lot, your yesterday is not what you remember.

Dr. Elizabeth Loftus, a cognitive psychologist, law professor, and author, speaks to how incorrect even our most basic memories are. After studying memory for more than forty years, she compares our memory to a Wikipedia page: anyone can go back and make edits.

In this case, the clickbait of reminiscing sounds a lot like Michael Scott explaining Wikipedia. "Wikipedia is the best thing ever. Anyone in the world can write anything they want about any subject, so you know you're getting the best possible information."

Man, oh man, that sounds like the conversations in our heads, doesn't it? The voice that tells us yesterday was better or that we were better yesterday speaks with so much authority, as if it has the best possible information! But it doesn't. It's got false information. It's dubious information; it shouldn't be relied on.

I've always found comfort in 1 John 3:20, specifically the last phrase: "For whenever our heart condemns us, God is greater than our heart, and He knows everything."

It's pretty crazy to me that this verse ends that way. "And He knows everything." It always seems a little out of place to me. The first part of this verse initially made me think of the heart as a bully. But God is bigger than all bullies, and He will fight for us! Sometimes your heart tries to bully you, but God will defend you even from your heart. I fully believe that is the truth, but I think there's even deeper truth in this specific verse. The last part of this verse shifts the entire picture.

The Greek word for "heart" is *kardia*. While it can mean the actual organ, it's also used to describe a person's soul. But the most meaningful definition is this: "the middle or central or inmost part of anything." I believe this verse is telling you and I that even if our inmost parts, the deepest parts of us that we can't even understand, stand against us and condemn us, God is greater than that. And it is He that knows everything, not your *kardia*. The deepest parts of you don't have all of the information. They don't know everything. God does!

GOD KNOWS THE ANSWERS TO ALL OF YOUR WHAT-IFS.

God knows the answers to all of your what-ifs. He literally knows what if, because he knows *everything*! He knows all the little intricacies and minor details of everything and penned your story before you ever breathed your first breath. He not only knew you'd be in this spot, on this day, but He went before you and made sure this place had everything you'd need to get everything He's made available for you! So we fix our eyes forward and pursue it.

Proverbs 4:23–26 sums up all of this quite nicely.

Keep your heart with all vigilance, for from it flow the springs of life. [24] *Put away from you crooked speech, and put devious talk far from you.*

[25] Let your eyes look directly forward, and your gaze be straight before you. [26] Ponder the path of your feet; then all your ways will be sure.

Like my mom says, "Don't look back! If you look back to remember, make sure it's wrapped up in gratitude!"

THE FINE PRINT

KNOW: God was good then, He'll be good tomorrow too!

LOOK OUT FOR: Feeling trapped between a fleeting, great yesterday and a terrifying tomorrow.

REMEMBER: God is greater than your heart, and He knows *everything*.

DO: Enjoy today, it's all you've got!

Does that really apply to you?

CHAPTER 5

THE CLICKBAIT OF SELF-DIAGNOSIS

Have you ever wondered why and how Doubting Thomas got his name? Well, obviously, you may be thinking, because he doubted. Thomas doubted, so he's called Doubting Thomas. Pretty cut-and-dried! Except that we don't call Peter "Doubting Peter" after he looked at the waves and sank. We don't call him "Denying Peter" even though he denied Jesus three times. So why does Thomas have that name?

I was shocked to find that Jesus didn't even refer to what Thomas did—needing to see the holes in Christ's hands before he would believe—as doubting. He didn't even say, "Oh, Thomas, why did you doubt?" No, that quote belongs to Peter's interaction on the waves with Jesus (Matthew 14:31). So why Thomas?

Thomas is never even referred to as Doubting Thomas in the Scriptures! The monks who put the subtitles and numbers into the Bible in the 1200s didn't even call him Doubting Thomas. And yet he is rarely referred to without his nickname, Doubting Thomas. Why is that?

I don't have *the* answer for it, but I have *an* answer: it's easier to label people. It's much easier to fathom everything about someone when they have a simple label. There are a lot of people to know, and a lot of things that make them who they are, and hundreds of thousands of micro decisions they make every single day as they create who they're becoming. It's way easier to slap a label on all that! And so Thomas is known as Doubting Thomas. This label helps us know his story before we ever even hear it. It's quite convenient!

I'm not against labels—most of them, anyway. I think most labels help our society function in a very positive way. We need to be able to search for "restaurant" on the internet and get a list of several establishments that serve food, even though none of them are actually called "restaurant." I need to be able to determine whether this shirt I'm looking at buying was made for a boy or a girl, someone my size or someone smaller, and how much this item will cost before I get to the register. We need to label every single piece of land, from the dividing lines of nations to the exact address you live in, so we can move and operate and get where we want to go. We need names so people can identify us from the rest of the crowd. Labels genuinely help!

And we all have labels. Everything has a name. As we grow and go through life, we begin to carry different labels, like Thomas. Labels like introvert and extrovert, Christian or Muslim, smart or dumb, and the like. Some are more harmless than others. Some are fair, and others are completely unfounded. Some labels are hot buzzwords, and some are old-school. We've all had, and will continue to have, to deal with the labels we seem to pick up over time. It's a part of life!

LABELS AREN'T DEFINITIONS, THEY'RE JUST SHORTCUTS.

When it comes to labels though, we make the mistake of thinking they're anything more than what they are: a simple label. They make life easier. They simplify, but they don't help us understand something in its entirety. They are not the be-all and end-all. They aren't God Himself. Labels aren't definitions, they're just shortcuts.

Labels can be harmful when people act like they define a person. But even more harmful than that is when a person turns the label maker around and labels themselves. It's harder at that point to believe a label is anything less than a complete definition of every aspect of who you are.

Therein lies the next very real clickbait tactic we will look at in this chapter: self-diagnosis. We all struggle with taking stock of our symptoms and shooting out a poorly researched and uneducated diagnosis. We all label ourselves. The average observer would count this type of behavior as mostly harmless until they read Proverbs 23:7 (KJV): "For as he thinketh in his heart, so is he." If that wasn't enough, there's Proverbs 18:21: "Death and life are in the power of the tongue, and those who love it will eat its fruits."

What we choose to think and say about ourselves carries more weight than an 18-wheeler. This is where we find that our voice is really what creates our world. We have everything God has ever said and promised available to us, but our tongue has the ability to create Hell on Earth.

In a world full of labels, our enemy throws everything he can at us to get us to believe these labels define everything about who we are. Our enemy uses the clickbait of self-diagnosis because we have the power to create our own worst nightmare with a few simple words.

Your friend has probably given into the clickbait of self-diagnosis if they say something like:

- "I'm just the type of person that ..."
- "I've just never really been into that."
- "I've always struggled with ..."

These statements, and any other that makes you think you have all the information about yourself, play right into the enemy's hand. He uses our own words against us, and he uses our voice to create a world no one would want. Christians have the power to speak into existence the things that are not, and the enemy harnesses that power to get us to self-define and self-diagnose. We, sadly, speak into existence things that are *not*.

WATCH OUT FOR FRISBEES

When Solomon says life and death are in the power of our tongue in Proverbs 18, I don't think he was saying our tongue is the most powerful organ. I don't think the power he is communicating only comes from our verbal communication.

Let me explain. I don't believe people can curse you. I don't think every word we say takes on life, even if we were joking. I've caught myself making a dark joke before only to quickly repent in my head just in case that joke sets into motion a horrible future I desperately don't want, but I don't think it actually works that way.

It's less about what's being said and more about what we're convinced of enough to actually say out loud. The enemy's work here isn't trying to get us to say stupid things we don't mean because those words don't have any power. His work is to get us to believe tiny, seemingly insignificant, self-limiting thoughts that have no place in the life of a child of God.

Just like David knew that his enemy was really coming against God, our beliefs about ourselves are actually beliefs about God. If we are His creation, then every thought we think about His creation has implications on what we believe about Him! A child of God that operates in self-limiting thoughts doesn't realize they are limiting their Father. If I am a limited child, that means my Father is limited in His ability. The danger in self-limiting thoughts isn't even in how it limits us, but how it limits Him!

So what does the enemy do? He hides in that fourth voice, that voice in your head, and lifts up arguments and opinions on everything you ever do. Since that voice is in our head, we believe they are our thoughts. Once we believe they are our thoughts, we think they are ours to fight off.

Let me demonstrate. If you have a weird thought, you have these two thoughts at once: "that thought was weird" and "I'm weird for having that thought." If someone was to ask you, "Have you ever had a weird thought like this?" you would say, "yes." You now consider yourself to be someone who has had that thought. Before you know it, you've diagnosed yourself as someone who has had those thoughts. Once the inner self-diagnosis takes place, it's not long before you feel as if you're the only one dealing with that thought process. Add all that to a society who loves to simplify everything into a few labels, and it's not long before you are a full-blown owner and operator of what was once a random and weird thought.

Instead of taking every thought captive and making it obedient to Christ, we somehow are taken captive by every thought and made to be obedient to it.

I don't think much of this is our fault, though. It's how we're wired. Part of this wiring can be explained in Jordan Peterson's description of our understanding of chaos and order.

Instead of taking every thought captive and making it obedient to Christ, we somehow are taken captive by every thought and made to be obedient to it.

> *Order and chaos are not understood first, objectively (as things or objects), and then personified. That would only be the case if we perceived objective reality FIRST, and then inferred intent and purpose. But that isn't how perception operates, despite our preconceptions. Perceptions of things as tools for example, occur before or in concert with perceptions of things as objects.* **We see what things mean just as fast or faster than we see what they are.**[1]

To explain this further, imagine you're minding your own business in the park and a couple of strangers are throwing around a frisbee a few yards away. Out of nowhere, the wind catches the frisbee and takes it in your direction. From the corner of your eye, you sense that something is coming at your head! You duck before you know what's actually coming at you. Your instincts knew it was time to duck before they even knew why. Your mind said "danger" before it said "frisbee."

We perceive what things mean faster than we perceive what they are. So when a random thought appears in the back of your head, a thought reaction goes off. You have the thought, and think that was weird, and wonder where it came from, and wonder if that makes you someone who has that thought, and wonder what in the world you're going to do now that you're that type of person that has that thought.

In other words, you rarely ever have just one thought at a time. Two thoughts, if not more, hit you at the same time. We see what the thought *means* even faster than we see what the thought *is*. We see the disease even faster than we see the symptom.

Then, instead of labeling the thought or even the action, we label ourselves (and other people too, but that's a different conversation for another day). It becomes an identity game. Instead of dealing with anxiety in the moment, we believe we are someone who deals with anxiety. Instead of admitting that was a mistake, we think we are the mistake. Instead of recognizing that it didn't work, we believe we don't work.

Even in the midst of all of this, we still aren't in the real danger zone yet. We enter it when we buy into all of this and sacrifice something of

1 Peterson, J. B. (2020). "12 Rules for Life: An Antidote to Chaos." pp. 38–39. Vintage Canada.

value in order to operate within this way of thinking. Whenever that voice in your head throws around a bunch of nonsense, the temptation is to use your voice to speak it into existence.

When the weight of all the thoughts that have taken you captive start to weigh too heavily, we search for any way to lighten the load. Labels make everything easier, so even in our pursuit of getting help, we end up labeling ourselves. We simplify our problem into a label to make it easier for people to understand what's going on!

When we don't know what's wrong with us, we call ourselves depressed! It's easier to simplify every aspect of what we're feeling into a label. Whenever we feel anxious, we say that we're a very anxious person. It communicates just about everything we'd want someone to know, from expectations of us to how to treat us, in a simple little label.

It's almost as if we feel peace on the other side of buying into the label. Even if we want to fight the label, we may believe the lie that labeling is the first step to defeating it. But labeling ourselves subconsciously turns it into an identity game, and that's a game we're going to lose.

LONELY TOWN

The whole point of the clickbait of self-diagnosis is to steal your identity. It's to take the label-maker out of God's hands and put it in your hands. It's to get people bound for Heaven in the next life to live out Hell on Earth in the meantime. It's to get us to stare into the face of the exceeding, abundant, and above-all-we-could-ever-ask-or-imagine God and choose what's behind door number two—not because we don't want Him, but because He could never really want us.

Self-diagnosis gets Christians to continue bearing the burdens that Christ has been begging to carry for them. It keeps Christians from reading their Bibles because how could someone like them even bear to read it? It lets people serve God's house but condemns them until they leave their harvest in the fields.

Now this is where the peanut gallery comes in and says, "Doesn't having a thought like that make you someone who has thoughts like that? You're not buying into a label, you're stating the facts!"

Yes, having certain thoughts does technically make you someone who deals with thoughts like that, on a certain level of analysis. But there are two things wrong with that belief.

First, you have absolutely no way of knowing if anyone else, or even everyone, is dealing with those exact same thoughts. You cannot search the minds of every Christian that has ever lived and determine if your case is normal or abnormal. But considering our population is over seven billion and continues to go up, I think it's fair to undoubtedly say that your battle is not unique to you.

Second, that level of analysis has a lesser understanding of identity, how it works, and the purposes it serves. That level completely ignores God's truth, and not in some simple way.

The Oxford Dictionary has two different definitions of "identity." As broken human beings, we naturally relate to the first one: "the characteristics determining who or what a person is." This is self-diagnosis. Even though we're limited beings with limited experiences who admittedly don't like ourselves very much, we all take the bait of this form of identity. We believe our characteristics make us who we are.

The second definition of identity is more appropriate for us Christians: "serving to establish who the holder, owner, or wearer is by bearing their name and often other details such as a signature or photograph." This level of analysis, this way of viewing identity, is more in line with God's truth. All of Scripture referencing who you are in Christ falls into place when you view your identity through this lens.

If we view ourselves as a collection of random characteristics, which that are mostly a product of our environment and are subject to change, then our identity will always be a moving target. We'll actually aid our enemy in his games by incorrectly saying, "God made me that way," in reference to a certain grouping of our characteristics.

But consider the psychology behind birth order in children. Psychologists have described "syndromes" that describe a similar collection of characteristics between people who are the firstborn child of their family, those who are middle-born, and even those who are only children. They have determined that most firstborn children share similar characteristics, like being typically more responsible and conscientious, looking to spend more time with adults than other kids. The environment that comes with being the first child of a couple, regardless of who that couple is, develops similar characteristics in firstborns.

Second or middle-born children tend to be annoyed with the responsible, almost parent-like firstborn. They tend to be more bold, rebellious, and exhibit an "ask for forgiveness, not permission" mentality (which makes us firstborns shudder at the thought). If characteristics like these are similar across different families, then to list our characteristics to describe how God made us is to set a very low bar for God's creativity. You are not your characteristics. You can't be!

We cannot jive with the first definition; we can only operate within the second. This first definition says, "I'm the brand." The second says, "He's the brand. I'm just the carrier." Think about it this way. If I wear an Adidas shirt, I'm not claiming to *be* Adidas. I'm just someone partaking in the brand and the products they supply. In the same way, as a Christian, I'm not claiming to *be* anything; I'm just someone partaking in God and the blessings He supplies!

YOU ARE NOT YOUR CHARACTERISTICS.

Understanding identity in this way clears everything up for us. Remember Genesis 1:27: "So God created man in His own image, in the image of God He created Him; male and female He created them."

We are made in His image; He is not made in ours. That means if He is not fearful, then we are not fearful. If He is not anxious, then we aren't anxious. If He isn't, we aren't! I'm not saying we are everything He is, but we can't be something He is not. For example, I have the DNA that my parents and grandparents carry. I may not be everything they are, but I can't have something they are not. I can't have DNA from someone else. In the same way, I may not be everything God is—but I'm definitely not something He isn't!

We may be broken, yes. But He has redeemed us, bringing value back to what was once broken. We are not only restored and back on the shelf, but we have a price tag. We are of value.

If the enemy can get you thinking you are a collection of your characteristics, that you are the brand, then you're open to condemnation.

You're the driver, the leader, and the ultimate decision-maker. That means you have to answer all the questions, and you'd better have good answers. Couple that with what Jeremiah says is an evil and deceitful heart (Jeremiah 17:9), and now you're outmanned living in lonely town. It's two against one. But when we remember that we are not the brand, nor are we the main character in our story, then we realize all accusations coming at us are actually accusing the brand-maker. They aren't coming at us; they're trying to come at Him.

And while you and I may be open to condemnation, He is not. In fact, the accuser and condemner knows not to try and accuse or condemn our God because he stands condemned before Him! Jesus condemned the ultimate condemner at the cross.

We fight off the clickbait of self-diagnosis by looking at Jeremiah 1: 17–19:

> [17] *But you, dress yourself for work; arise, and say to them everything that I command you. Do not be dismayed by them, lest I dismay you before them.* [18] *And I, behold, I make you this day a fortified city, an iron pillar, and bronze walls, against the whole land, against the kings of Judah, its officials, its priests, and the people of the land.* [19] *They will fight against you, but they shall not prevail against you, for I am with you, declares the Lord, to deliver you.*

They will fight, but they will not prevail!

POINTING AND CALLING

The Japanese railway station is known for one of the seemingly most bizarre practices in the industry. They have a system known as pointing and calling. Each worker on the railway has been given some sort of task, and when it comes time, they will point and call out that task. The conductor will point and call out the exact speed when they arrive at their top speed. They will point at the speedometer when they've come to a complete stop and call out the speed. The workers at each door will each point and call out "All clear!" when they're ready to take off again. This simple system has reduced errors by 85 percent.

> JESUS CONDEMNED THE ULTIMATE CONDEMNER AT THE CROSS.

As effective as that system has been for railway systems, I think it's even more effective in our battle against self-diagnosis. Instead of letting the thought take you captive, point and call it out for what it is. We point and call out the thoughts for what they are—thoughts. We say, "That's fear. That's manipulation. That's sin." Let's not label ourselves; let's label the thought!

Truth be told, I don't have all the answers. I don't know what thoughts you're battling with, what's seemingly pulling on you every day, or what any of that makes you. I don't even know what I'm battling with or what it makes me! But that's just it; it doesn't make me anything. It can't. I've already been made. And like we referenced in the last chapter, 1 John 3:20 tells us that it's God that actually knows everything. He's the one who has all the information. He's the one that created you, all of mankind, and all the different things that make us human. If there was anyone able to label you properly, it would be the creator of what is being labeled.

I find comfort in this. If He knows everything, that means I don't have to. And that's what you would need in order to correctly diagnose yourself; you'd have to be an expert in literally everything. The greatest doctors all over the world have studied portions of the body more than others have studied anything in their entire lives, and even they struggle with finding the correct diagnoses. We aren't experts in everything, let alone anything. We couldn't correctly self-diagnose even if we wanted to.

I've often been dumbfounded by some of Peter's closing remarks in 1 Peter 5. He's telling his audience to resist the devil as he's closing his first letter, and he says, "Resist him, firm in your faith, knowing that the same kinds of suffering are being experienced by your brotherhood throughout the world" (1 Peter 5:9).

It puzzles me because it makes the battle feel even larger. You mean to tell me everyone is going through this same thing?! But we're supposed to find comfort in this because it proves this battle is not unique to you. If it's not unique to you, then it can't be part of your identity.

You aren't a label, you are a son or daughter of the Living God!

THE FINE PRINT

KNOW: You are who God says you are.

LOOK OUT FOR: Feeling like an expert in anything.

REMEMBER: HE knows everything (notice the difference in emphasis).

REMEMBER (PART 2): The same things are being experienced by your brothers and sisters all over the world.

DO: Label the thought, not yourself!

God said He'd do it… but will He really? And how?

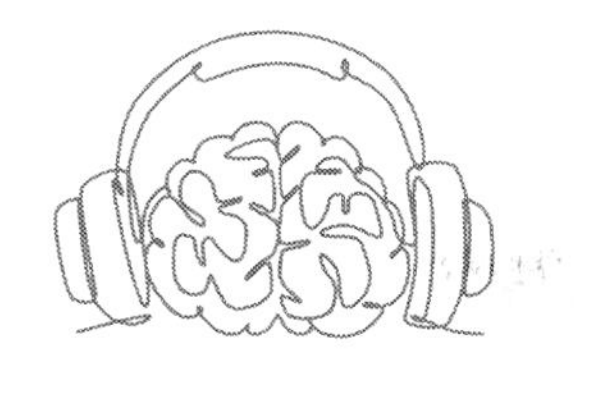

CHAPTER 6

THE CLICKBAIT OF "MAYBE"

Some may call my love for The Office an obsession. Those people would be right! In between working full-time as a pastor since I was twenty-four and going to college, I've found time to watch the entire series five or six times. To be entirely honest, I've lost count.

To make matters worse, I'm an enabler. Everyone in my world is experiencing their own obsession with the paper company in Scranton, Pennsylvania. We've even found ourselves assigning members of our friend group to each character, finding our own Dwights, Kevins, and Creeds. The cast is just too relatable!

This enabling bit me in the butt around the dinner table a while back, though. We were having a friendly discussion about who in our world had the most in common with Jim, as we were thinking of all dressing up as The Office cast for Halloween. I confidently believed I had the greatest cause to represent Jim, so I stood up and made my case. I was met with an eruption of laughter. "We already decided; you're Michael!"

There's nothing wrong with being Michael Scott, but it's all too easy to identify with the wrong character. We line up all the pieces into the puzzle we want to create, not the real picture on the box. We jump to the conclusion that we're dodging spears like David, when in reality we're flinging them like Saul. Many of us have thought we were stepping out in faith like Abram when we were actually running from faith like Jonah. I've seen tons of women overlook great dudes in their church because they're "waiting on their Boaz."

To modern Christians, the narrative of Abraham's life has almost become synonymous with the faith walk. It's as if we believe our lives will have the exact same components of his. As true as this may be in theory, we take this too far. Some people start searching for the Isaac they need to be willing to sacrifice. Some people assume they have to leave where they're planted to go and pursue "where God will show them," mistaking their season of crushing for their "get up and go" season.

We all think that we need to leave what we've known and pursue what God is showing us. We all think that we need to march up that mountain and sacrifice Isaac. And we're not wrong, we're absolutely right.

But while we're right in theory, we can still be totally wrong. I know it's hard to fathom, but even Christians can make wrong decisions. And we make those bad decisions because we buy into the clickbait of "maybe."

LIVING ON A MAYBE

We tend to read about Abraham's life like a social media page, we only catch the highlights. But this unbelievable man of faith had some low-lights too.

> *Now Sarai, Abram's wife, had borne him no children. She had a female Egyptian servant whose name was Hagar. [2] And Sarai said to Abram, "Behold now, the Lord has prevented me from bearing children. Go in to my servant; it may be that I shall obtain children by her." And Abram listened to the voice of Sarai. Genesis 16:1–2*

Those last few words give me the bad goosebumps. The father of our faith, the man referenced throughout the Old and New Testament countless times because he listened to the Lord, the man whose faith was credited to him as righteousness, listened to the voice of Sarai. God had promised to bring him a child through Sarai, and yet Abraham chose to listen to Sarai. How could this happen?

Just look at Sarai's statement to Abraham in verse 2; "it may be that I shall obtain children by her." It may be. *Maybe.* Abraham and Sarah had a direct promise from God, but they didn't know how He was going to do it. They were left with a "maybe" and plunged into a wrong decision.

They aren't alone in that. When we follow a maybe and buy into our plan, even with good intentions, we identify with the wrong character.

We think we're Abraham, but we're really Jonah. We think we're Jim, but we're actually Michael Scott.

The clickbait of "maybe" doesn't try to keep us from doing the right things, it baits us into doing the wrong things. The clickbait of "maybe" gets us listening to the wrong voice, the voice that sounds good. The clickbait of "maybe" tempts us to get the promise through means that make sense to us, or even to sacrifice the wrong Isaac.

You've probably taken the clickbait of "maybe" if you've said this recently:

- "Maybe I'm supposed to find a new church so I can really grow."
- "Maybe I'm supposed to quit my job so God can teach me to rely on Him."
- "Maybe I'm one of those people that don't need school."
- "Maybe I'm supposed to forget wisdom and counsel and act out in faith."
- "Maybe I'm supposed to struggle here so I have a greater testimony."

I know, I know, these sound harmless. But the clickbait of "maybe" brought Ishmael into the world, and look what was said of what his life would become:

> *He shall be a wild donkey of a man, his hand against everyone and everyone's hand against him, and he shall dwell over against all his kinsmen. Genesis 16:12*

Whenever we move on a "maybe," we are bringing something to life. Most of the time, whatever is birthed from a "maybe" ends up being wild and against everyone.

DOING IT WRONG

We've looked at Abraham and Sarah a bit, but this book is really about Eve. We've been looking at this short passage of Scripture throughout these chapters, about the thought process and challenges that led to Eve making the biggest mistake in human history. But eventually, no matter what the serpent said or what she was thinking about, she reached out and took the fruit. She heard a lot, she saw a lot, but none of that mattered until she reached out and took it.

The clickbait of "Maybe" gets us to reach out and take something that isn't for us. It makes us eat the wrong fruit. Think about what chapter 3 says; the fruit looked good, it was desirable to make one wise, and I'm pretty sure trying to be more like God isn't a bad thing! But obedience isn't about doing good things. Obedience isn't about doing the things you think God would get on board with. Obedience is doing only what God has told you, exactly when He's told you.

To be totally honest, I don't think the enemy has to work really hard with this clickbait. I think we do most of the work on this one. Not intentionally, obviously. But even Scripture concedes that this will be a problem for us.

We looked at Isaiah 43:19 already, but let's look again; "Behold, I am doing a new thing; now it springs forth, do you not perceive it? I will make a way in the wilderness and rivers in the desert."

OBEDIENCE IS DOING ONLY WHAT GOD HAS TOLD YOU, EXACTLY WHEN HE'S TOLD YOU.

Those looking for a verse that says "God will make a way when there is no way" will be shocked to know it doesn't exist. That idea is actually taken from this verse in Isaiah. God is telling the people of Israel that He's doing something new, and it's already underway. But He recognizes they're having trouble perceiving it. So what does God say? He says He will literally make a way in the wilderness and make rivers in the desert. He will make both a way out and a source of sustenance to keep them until they get out!

But we struggle to perceive all that God is doing, so we pull on a "maybe." We play out the scenarios, pick the one we can get on board with the most, and head in that direction. God has promised to make the way, but we lunge forward and try to make one ourselves. When we make the way, we've failed before we've even embarked on our journey.

How do we avoid this? How do we avoid being Eve, desiring wisdom by making unwise choices? How do we ensure we hear God, and we're not hanging on a "maybe"?

We start by trying to define one of the more loosely defined terms in all of Scripture: faith. As Christians, we tend to throw around some statements every single day without knowing what they really mean. We hear and say things like "the righteous live by faith" and "Christianity isn't a religion, it's a relationship" all the time without fully understanding what those phrases mean. Even though Hebrews 11 breaks down what faith is, it's still very difficult to flesh out what faith is and what faith isn't. So we naturally tend to think faith and "maybe" are somewhat synonymous.

We look at Peter walking on the uncertainty of water and call that faith. We then say that walking on anything uncertain must be faith too! But this couldn't be further from the truth. Let's look to the Bibles actual definition of faith: "Now faith is the assurance of things hoped for, the conviction of things not seen" (Hebrews 11:1).

Do you see any maybes in there? Other versions of this verse replace "conviction" with the word "evidence." How many criminals get convicted because of a "maybe?" How long will a "maybe" stand up in court?

"Maybe" does not equal faith. "Maybe" weighs options and chooses the one it feels most comfortable with. "Maybe" plays out the movie and picks the ending it likes the most. "Maybe" says, "I see how God can use that, so let's do it!"

Where is the faith in that?

Faith is being certain that if we do our part, God will do His—even when we can't see it. Faith says, "I'm going!" not, "I'm running." Faith says, "I know God is doing something new, even if I can't perceive it!"

"Maybe" is building our house on the sand. "Maybe" is not doubling your talents, but burying them. On the other hand, faith is being led, not being driven.

LED, NOT DRIVEN

Abraham had lowlights, but even still he's one of the greatest examples of faith in all of Scripture. He listened to the voice of God. He was told to go. He didn't leave everything he knew to pursue a "maybe." He didn't weigh his options after hearing God speak and realize it would be good for him and Sarah. He wasn't running away from something, he was running

"MAYBE" DOES NOT EQUAL FAITH.

to something. God's goal pushed him out of comfort to where he needed to be. But too many times we use this story so we can run away from the uncomfortable today to pursue the "maybe."

I really believe Abraham would have scoffed at the thought of leaving the day before God told him to leave. Abraham looked at leaving just like Jonah looked at going: they both probably said, "I can't." Jonah thought "I can't" meant "it's not God." But for Abraham, he knew "I can't" meant "it has to be God."

Here's the issue with "maybe" thinking: it leaves way too much room for you. There is a big I in "maybe." There's no I in "faith." (Well, except for the literal "i" in "faith.")

We live in a time where it's good to be driven. We are a goal-oriented society where you're encouraged to define your end goal and live every day in pursuit of that end goal. So we put extra work in because we're driven by this end goal. But I'm not sure how Biblical that is. I don't hear Paul giving a lesson on goal setting in any of his letters. You never hear Jesus asking someone, "Hey, where do you see yourself in five years?" I have nothing against this type of thinking, but I do have an issue with making it equal to the gospel.

Abraham didn't leave because of the potential opportunity. He didn't leave because it lined up with his goals. He left because he was led by his principles, one of them being "when God speaks, I listen." He listened even when it meant leaving and wondering. Even when it meant discomfort.

You and I aren't meant to be driven by our goals and desires; we're meant to be led by our principles. A principle is a cause-and-effect relationship. If I do this, then this will happen. If I do my part, I know God will do His part. If He's promised to make a way in the desert, then I can operate on this principle: "they that wait on the Lord shall have their strength renewed." (Isaiah 40:31)

The book of Proverbs gives us hundreds of other principles to operate in that simplify every major decision we could ever face. For instance, if you're wondering if you're in the right spot, consider this: "Without counsel plans fail, but with many advisers they succeed" (Proverbs 15:22). Get wise counsel! Or if you're wondering if you're with the "right" person, consider:

"Do not be unequally yoked with unbelievers" (2 Corinthians 6:14). If you put those two things together, you'll solve 90 percent of your issues.

Here are some others I live by:

- If I stay planted and water the grass I'm on, my grass will get greener.
- If I take care of God's house, He will take care of mine.
- Seed, time, and harvest; everything will start with a seed, it'll take time, and I'll see a harvest.

Living a life of faith is hard, but principles make it easier. We could go on and on about combating each "maybe" with a different biblical principle, but this is only one chapter, and we've got a lot more to get to. So when you catch yourself getting overwhelmed with "maybes," connect with a biblical authority figure you trust—a pastor, a leader, or a parent—and spill all your "maybes" to them. All of them. Spend more time asking your spiritual authority how you should be thinking, not what you should be doing. Don't say, "what should I do?" Ask, "What should I be thinking?"

This type of submission of thought helps you take every thought captive, making it obedient to Jesus. This practice will also make the next clickbait much easier to face as well.

THE FINE PRINT

KNOW: Obedience is greater than sacrifice.

LOOK OUT FOR: The temptation to think movement equals progress.

REMEMBER: God is principled!

DO: Be led by principles, not driven by goals!

@YourEnemy

Do they really know what you're going through?

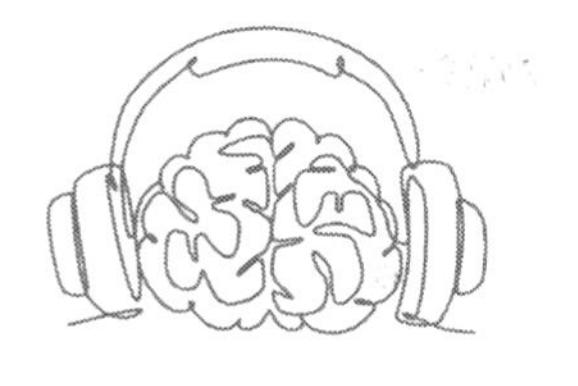

CHAPTER 7

THE CLICKBAIT OF SELF-PITY

I wonder what it must be like to exist in a world with one other human being, surrounded by thousands of animals. They were severely outnumbered. They were tasked with tending to the land and the animals, so they had a front row seat to the absolute beauty of each and every creature. I don't know if Eve ever would have compared herself to any of the animals, but I do wonder what it must have felt like to question God for the very first time. I wonder what it felt like to hear that God may be holding out on you, or to hear that He's afraid of being on equal footing with you.

I have to imagine there was a significant moment of introspection between verses 5 and 6 of Genesis 3. For a single moment, Eve was presented with the thought that she could have better. She didn't really know if it would end up being better, but the thought of her becoming more than what she was consumed her.

I don't know if I blame her. Would you look at an opportunity to be more than you are, and pass on it? Would you leave that moment and go back to whatever you were before that opportunity to be more came about? Probably not. Once we feel the grass is greener somewhere else, it's hard to not hate the grass you're standing on.

And then, to make matters worse, she was presented with the idea that it was God who was holding her back from this. Like the great movie Inception says, "An idea is the most resilient parasite." Can you imagine having to go back to normal life with this thought hanging around in

“

Once we feel the grass is greener somewhere else, it's hard to not hate the grass you're standing on.

the back of your head, that God was keeping you from more? How do you enjoy a single second of your life if you feel like God is keeping you from more?

I know this is an overdramatization of those verses, but our enemy knows that we have a tendency to look down on our current scenario once we think that there's more. It's hard to enjoy paradise if you feel there's a better paradise out there.

This isn't a reference to pursuing more for your life, like a better job, a healthier lifestyle, etc. This refers to the countless times we believe we deserve better from our family, our friends, our leaders, and even God. This is a reference to the many times that we feel unworthy of the problems we face, and we blame the people and the God that we hold responsible for those problems.

It's called self-pity, and it's one of the most dangerous forms of clickbait in our enemy's arsenal.

By now you've noticed a lot of these chapters start with being perplexed by certain Bible stories. There's a lot to wonder about when we look at the lives of those found in the Bible. But if this were a yearbook, "most likely to perplex" would have to go to Elijah.

If 1 Kings 18 and 19 were pictures, they'd paint Elijah's candidacy for "most likely to perplex" perfectly. The first picture, 1 Kings 18, would be of an incredible man on top of a mountain with his hands stretched toward the heavens. Lightning would be striking all throughout the skies. You'd see fire falling from Heaven as hundreds of other people run away.

The second picture, 1 Kings 19, would be a lowly man in the fetal position in an elaborate, dark cave. His fear is almost tangible, as he'd be rocking himself to sleep in this dark cave.

The scary part about these two images is that each picture is of the same man. In one picture, he is victorious while everyone else runs. In the second, he's completely alone and afraid.

How does this happen? How is he painted so strong in one picture and so weak in the next? How does someone call for God to end their life just days after calling down fire from Heaven? How did he have so much confidence in God's ability that he would challenge four hundred false prophets and then forget all of God's ability hours later? What can do this to such a man?

I've had different answers to this question throughout my life, but the answer has become clear in the last few years. It's not simply the ups and downs of ministry, as I have believed from time to time. It's not simply a Christian's everyday battle with depression, as I have also believed from time to time. I believe the answer is something much simpler.

Self-pity.

"Excessive, self-absorbed unhappiness over one's own troubles," as the Oxford Dictionary puts it. Obsessing over your own problems. The only way I can understand Elijah's fall from chapter 18 to 19 is when I consider that he genuinely, wholeheartedly, believed Jezebel's threat. Even though she swore by her own gods—the gods Elijah just exposed—he had to be obsessing over this threat. He was at the end of his rope, completely worn out, with nothing left. And it's all thanks to self-pity.

The clickbait of self-pity sounds like this:

- "Do you really think anyone else has it this hard?"
- "You're only one person, and you have to protect yourself."
- "How could a good God let this happen?"

The hard part about the clickbait of self-pity is it's not really wrong; each statement makes some level of sense. Adam and Eve would have a heightened sense of good and evil if they ate the fruit, and God did definitely know that. But what's wrong about these statements is what we allow them to imply, to become, and to grow into.

Elijah did feel alone, but that didn't mean he *was* alone. You may feel like this is really hard, but that doesn't mean it's *too* hard. You are only one person, but that doesn't mean you are *limited*! Especially with God. This situation may have you questioning the goodness of God, but that doesn't mean He *isn't* good.

Self-pity, an obsession over your own problems, takes the man off the mountain and puts him in the cave by his own hand. Self-pity ruins relationships not just between men and women, but between a man and himself. Self-pity is a gateway drug, opening the door to a depression that calls into question everything you believe. Self-pity makes even the greatest victories inconsequential and insignificant.

And yet, as dangerous as it is, we all find ways to obsess over our own problems. Like the clickbait of self-diagnosis, our enemy uses self-pity to take our eyes off of God and put them onto ourselves. Self-pity specializes in taking us from the highest heights to the lowest lows, somehow convincing us that our problems are significantly worse than everyone else's. Self-pity can convince anyone that withholding a tree is unfair, even though we have an entire paradise at our disposal.

SELF-PITY MAKES EVEN THE GREATEST VICTORIES INCONSEQUENTIAL AND INSIGNIFICANT.

I know this can seem dramatic, especially to someone who may be currently fighting off the clickbait of self-pity. But when you consider how much self-pity drastically changed Elijah's two pictures, you quickly realize anything powerful enough to send a man like Elijah into a suicidal fit is worth taking seriously.

KEEPING SCORE

If we're going to see self-pity for the true killer that it is, and if I'm going to say it's the main reason Elijah fell so far from his great heights, then we're going to need to locate it in his story. We need to see where Elijah may have obsessed over his own troubles. So let's go back to the beginning, the story before the story.

> *After many days the word of the Lord came to Elijah, in the third year, saying, "Go, show yourself to Ahab, and I will send rain upon the earth."* [2] *So Elijah went to show himself to Ahab. Now the famine was severe in Samaria.* [3] *And Ahab called Obadiah, who was over the household. (Now Obadiah feared the Lord greatly,* [4] *and when Jezebel cut off the prophets of the Lord, Obadiah took a hundred prophets and hid them by fifties in a cave and fed them with bread and water.)* [5] *And Ahab said to*

Obadiah, "Go through the land to all the springs of water and to all the valleys. Perhaps we may find grass and save the horses and mules alive, and not lose some of the animals." [6] *So they divided the land between them to pass through it. Ahab went in one direction by himself, and Obadiah went in another direction by himself.* [7] *And as Obadiah was on the way, behold, Elijah met him. And Obadiah recognized him and fell on his face and said, "Is it you, my lord Elijah?"* [8] *And he answered him, "It is I. Go, tell your lord, 'Behold, Elijah is here.'" 1 Kings 18:1–8*

1 Kings 18 starts with Obadiah, the prophet who has his own book of the Bible later in the Old Testament. Obadiah finds himself in captivity, as he's been taken by Ahab and Jezebel. Ahab sent out a decree to kill all the prophets of the Lord, so Obadiah leaps into action and hides away a hundred other prophets in the caves. He's partially the reason Elijah is still alive, as he has been tasked with finding Elijah. Once they find him, Ahab will kill them both.

They finally run into each other in verse 7, bringing Obadiah to his most bittersweet reality. We read their conversation in verses 7–15, ending right before Elijah's greatest mountaintop moment (literally). Then we fast forward to our second picture, as Elijah is now begging for some type of spiritual euthanasia. He says:

I have been very jealous for the Lord, the God of hosts. For the people of Israel have forsaken your covenant, thrown down your altars, and killed your prophets with the sword, **and I, even I only, am left**, *and they seek my life, to take it away. 1 Kings 19:10*

Here Elijah believes he is the only prophet left, but didn't he just meet Obadiah one chapter earlier? Didn't Obadiah just tell Elijah that he had hid another a hundred prophets? One hundred plus one equals at least another 101 prophets! And yet Elijah believes he's the only prophet left. He completely disregarded Obadiah and all the work he had done. It gets even more strange when you keep reading chapter 19 to find that God tells Elijah that He has stored away seven *thousand* others who have not turned away from Him. We hear of another one as Elijah is about to be sent to anoint his successor!

That brings our running total of prophets to at least 7,102. That's a long way away from being the only one left. But that didn't matter to Elijah. He completely dismissed Obadiah, the hundred prophets he hid, and everything else God was working on. He was completely obsessed with his own problems and took the clickbait of self-pity. He clicked the link and signed up for the newsletter.

Self-pity took Elijah from the mountaintop to a cave, but it wasn't a one-time decision. No one ever takes the clickbait of self-pity out of nowhere. There is always a series of microdecisions that lead to constantly obsessing over your own problems.

I call that paper trail "keeping score." We all keep score. This truth is easier to swallow when we focus on other people, so let's stick to talking about them for a bit. We all know people that keep score, that walk around with invisible scorecards backed by their own grading scale, keeping track of what everyone is doing to them and everything they are doing for others.

You know these types of people. They're the people who give gifts so they can get gifts. My dad calls that a "gift for a gift" gift. These people don't know it, but they're secretly reading into all of your actions, assuming you're thinking of them deliberately with each step. Some people say "no strings attached"; these people have strings attached to everything.

I, too, keep score. It's one of my biggest battles. I didn't know I struggled with keeping score until my mom pointed it out one fateful day. I had helped my dad around his property in Georgia all day, and I had finally showered up and sank into the couch ready to relax. He came around the corner, happy as all get out, and made one more request. I felt like I had done enough that day, and so I said no. I told myself that I had said yes nine times, so it would be okay to say no once.

A fight ensued. Not only between my dad and I, but it really got heated with my mom. I'd never yell at my mom, but she did a lot of yelling that day! Why? Because no one likes to do life with someone who keeps score. Not simply because it's unfair, but because it eventually makes you delusional. When we keep score, we are not simply keeping score with our fellow humans; we are ultimately keeping score with God.

Enter Elijah. Elijah kept score. He *really* kept score. It's clear in his conversation with God. Read 1 Kings 19:10 from earlier again, but this time imagine he's holding an invisible scorecard. Do you see him developing the different teams? "I'm good, but your people aren't." And then he doubles down on this belief in verse 14! He retweeted himself. Here this man thought he could accurately judge life and felt the need to remind God of what was going on, as if God doesn't see everything. As if God doesn't know everything. Can you imagine the pride you must have to feel like you have to give God a report of how things are going down here?

But that's what keeping score does; it creates a perfect ledger that God must atone for. You're saying, "I deserve more, and God should repay me."

But no one can keep an accurate ledger. Elijah believed he had been jealous before the Lord, and yet he completely overlooked Obadiah. He heard Obadiah's story about the bravery it took to hide away a hundred other prophets and threw it out. He was keeping score incorrectly. As he believed he deserved more because of all he had done right, he was overlooking his own sin.

The clickbait of self-pity specializes in causing us all to overlook Obadiahs. Whenever we catch ourselves taking the bait of self-pity, we have to acknowledge that we've been keeping score and doing it wrong. Not only have we overlooked Obadiah, but our math doesn't add up either.

PROMISES, PROMISES

As Christians, our entire faith walk is founded on principles that are polar opposite to self-pity. We are taught to love others and put their needs first. We are taught that trouble is part of the process, but that Christ has already overcome it. We are taught that giving is better than receiving, that justice is the Lord's, and that He promises to make everything turn out for our good.

We are taught a lot more too:

- He promises to restore the joy of our salvation.
- He promises to complete the good work that He started in us.
- He declares He is doing a new thing, and that He is making a way in the wilderness and streams in the desert.

We are taught that God is more than enough for us, that He is King of Kings and Lord of Lords. He is able to do above all we could ever ask or imagine, exceedingly and abundantly. He is good and where our help comes from. He is our defender and our provider, our savior and our friend. He is perfect and all powerful. He is the God of all comfort. He is strong when we are weak, and worthy of all the praise we can give. He saved us. He sent Jesus for us. He died for us. He has forgiven us! He had called us! He sent us His Spirit!

He sees us, hears us, and knows us. He says nothing, in all creation, will ever be able to separate us from His love in Christ Jesus. He says we are the victor, not a victim. He promises us that He is always in control. His faithfulness is a shield about us! He wants to lead us beside the still waters and give us rest! He will renew our strength!

He's ordered our steps! He's declared the work finished! He says we are more than conquerors in Christ! And on top of all of that, He wants to give us the desires of our heart.

Now let me ask you, where is there any room for self-pity in all that?

This is why our enemy will deploy the clickbait of self-pity so often: because it flies in the face of everything our faith is founded on. It gets our eyes off of God and on to ourselves, and then we have a self-centered faith. Not just a selfish faith, but a faith that is literally based and centered around you. Self-centered faith isn't faith at all.

Genuine faith and self-pity are mutually exclusive. Jesus has already overcome the world, so how can we obsess over any problem, let alone our own? Whenever we obsess over our own problems, we say goodbye to the promises of God. Not because they cease to be true, but because we've elevated our problems above their truth.

Not only does self-pity fly in the face of God's truth, but it flies in the face of reality. I find my problems don't bear much weight when compared to the problems of doctors, members of our military, etc. Whenever I'm overwhelmed with my own problems, I ask myself these questions:

- What about the doctor that has to inform a family that their father didn't survive his heart attack?

“

Self-centered faith isn't faith at all.

”

- What about the police captains and chaplains that have to inform families that their fathers, mothers, brothers, aunts and uncles have died in the line of duty?
- What about the men and women running into the fires and natural disasters that we instinctively run away from?
- What about the war generals who have to send their troops into battle knowing it could be the end for some?

If that doesn't work, and I admit sometimes it doesn't, I ask myself these questions:

- Where is the victory in feeling sorry for myself?
- How do I win by obsessing over my problems?
- Even if all of what I'm feeling is true, how does dwelling on it help me?

There is no victory on the other side of self-pity. You don't win by feeling sorry for yourself. And this truth should excite us—not because life isn't hard or painful, but because so many people have done great things in the midst of pain and difficulty, and you can too!

We must learn to see our problems as obstacles to be overcome rather than giants standing in our way. When we realize everything coming against us is simply an obstacle, and we as Christians were made to overcome obstacles, then we will charge at every lion and bear, and eventually Goliath.

Do you realize we don't hear about any of David's good days as a shepherd? We only hear about the days where something came against him, whether it was being forgotten by his father, watching the lion and bear go after his sheep, or being left behind when his brothers went to war. We rarely hear about his good days as a king too! We hear a lot about his time on the run, or his mistakes with Bathsheba and the census. I'm not quite sure why, but one thing is clear; David was an overcomer!

And consider this last fact: if a warrior stands against you, it must mean he thinks you too are a warrior.

FIGHTING SELF-PITY

We said a lot about who God is in the last section. We listed God's promises, most of which are promises He makes about Himself. When I was writing all of that, faith swelled up in me. I believe faith swelled up in you too!

Maybe you skimmed that part, especially because Christians have heard so much of that before. But go back. Read it again. Slow down and take it line by line. Watch as faith swells up in your heart and mind! Then do it again and again. Get a pen out and start writing them down on your own. Turn some worship music on and recite the list as the song plays.

I have to admit, I probably would not do any of that if I was just reading this book. But I've learned in my short life that the only true way to combat the clickbait of self-pity is true, genuine worship. It's not simply playing worship music, although that's great! It's not just the opening portion of our church services. It's true recognition of who He is, what He says about Himself, and putting Him in His rightful seat as Lord of our lives.

David knew how to worship. We do mostly hear about his bad days, but the other book attributed to him is his book of Psalms—his worship. We know him as a warrior and a worshipper, not an adulterer and murderer. He was an overcomer because he knew how to worship He who has overcome the world!

That's why faith swelled up in me as I wrote that list, but that didn't surprise me. When I wrote the outline of this chapter, knowing I would write that section, I knew an elevated faith would accompany that part. That list of promises came straight out of my "Sermon to Myself," a document I wrote up years ago to combat my own battle with self-pity. Of all the clickbaits we've discussed, self-pity is the one I struggle with the most. At the height of my obsession, I decided to start each morning talking about who God is and what He says. It was an attempt to immediately make the day about Him and not about me.

This simple practice has changed everything for me. And I believe true, genuine worship will change everything for you too! I give every reader permission to stop reading to take a moment to truly worship the King of Kings and the Lord of Lords. Just recognizing that He truly is the King of Kings and Lord of Lords combats the temptation to feel sorry for yourself. If He really is King of Kings and Lord of Lords, and yet He promises little old me the desires of my heart, then all that's left to say is, "What is man that you are mindful of him, and the son of man that you care for him?" (Psalm 8:4)

True and genuine worship is the only way to put self-pity to rest. It's hard to obsess over a single problem when we remind ourselves of who God is. I've made the "Sermon to Myself" document fully available in the back of this book, but it should be your template. You need to write about who God is to you! Do a quick Google search on the promises of God and go to town. You'll see faith swell up in you faster than self-pity would let you believe is possible!

THE FINE PRINT

KNOW: You aren't alone in this!

LOOK OUT FOR: The temptation to keep score!

REMEMBER: We always lose when we keep score.

DO: Break the scorecard!

PART 3

THE SOLUTION

CHAPTER 8

FIGHTING CLICKBAIT

"Someone call the Hulk!" These were the confusing, albeit intriguing words my physical therapist shouted during my third session after I ruptured my Achilles' in 2017 while playing basketball. It was a complete tear, a total separation of the tendon from the bone. It felt like I had been shot. People playing on other courts told us they thought a gun had gone off. And yet as painful as that experience was, it did not compare in the slightest to what would follow my physical therapist's confusing exclamation.

Out walked a thin, short woman that hardly matched any mental image anyone would have of someone nicknamed the Hulk. She came over and introduced herself as she sat down before me, instructing me to turn over and lay on my stomach. I listened and made some type of sarcastic remark about the gap between reality and my expectation of her nickname, and she laughed and again instructed me to turn over and lay down. She began to run her knuckles up and down my Achilles', applying more and more force as she went along.

This relaxed me, so I finally heeded her full instructions and laid all the way down. Right as I started to believe I could take a quick nap, I felt the cold touch of metal on my incredibly sensitive, surgically repaired Achilles'. I had just met the Graston, the tool they would use to break up all the scar tissue.

The Hulk's nickname started to make sense as she ran this Graston all along my leg.

As I try to explain what happened next, and in the sessions that followed, all I can say is this: I did not cry. The Hulk actually congratulated me at the end of all of my sessions, saying I was one of the few people to complete this form of therapy without crying. If this explanation still doesn't satisfy you, feel free to Google the Graston technique and watch a few videos. You will quickly understand why the Hulk encouraged me to tap the table at any point if the pain became unbearable. She literally encouraged me to tap out.

I'm glad to say I never succumbed to this pressure, and I'm thankful they never charged me for the chunk of cushion I may or may not have bitten out of the therapy table.

Whenever I play basketball or go for a quick run, I'm thankful I never tapped out. I wouldn't be able to do either, or at least not in a decent manner, if I had tapped out and stopped short of completing the therapy. I remember doing everything I could to focus on anything but the pain! But man ... I was close. It became increasingly harder to process how so much pain was supposed to help me.

This is where my experience with the Hulk and her Graston meets our everyday life. The mind games of life and our battle against clickbait can get really painful. When it does, it's hard to fathom how this pain is supposed to help us. It's increasingly more difficult to know how fighting off so much that offends us, fighting the unhealthy side of reminiscing, walking the delicate balance of maybe, and refusing to feel sorry for ourselves, all while trying not to self-diagnose is somehow healthy for us. Just writing that sentence was hard, as I'm sure it's hard to read, let alone try to live out.

It's only human nature to equate this pain with something wrong, and then we become desperate to discover which wrong is causing this much pain. Our enemy, master of clickbait and the leader of these mind games, is quick to relay the message that if nothing is wrong with a perfect God, then there must be something wrong with you. Once you arrive at this conclusion, you believe something is wrong with *only* you. At that point, the only seemingly viable option is tapping out. Our only option is to ask for the pain to stop. To give up on hope. To give in to a certain label. To believe what "they" have been saying all along.

We tap out and end the fight because that's our only option, right?

TAG OUT, DON'T TAP OUT

In my first book, *Up Next*, I used a boxing analogy to describe the many decision fights in life. Sometimes we don't know if we "won" certain encounters or decisions for a very long time. In some areas, we won't really know until we get to Heaven! I'm not much of a fan of fighting sports, but I felt drawn to another fighting analogy here as we discuss the desire to tap out in this battle with clickbait.

A boxer is completely alone in the ring. They have people in their corner for support, but it's just them and the one opposing them out there once that bell rings. However, the battle for our minds is not a boxing match! We aren't alone out here. This battle is more like professional wrestling, the WWE fights. Now, I can't say I've watched many of these fights, but I have seen tons of commercials and videos on YouTube. Just about every one of these commercials show some clip of a fighter losing the fight (real or fake), but they turn to their teammate. That teammate climbs on the ropes and leaps toward their opponent, somehow landing only on the opponent (all while doing a few backflips or something) while his formerly losing teammate climbs out of the ring. He tagged out, and his teammate took over.

As funny as WWE can be, I do believe we can learn something from it: there's a significant difference in our fight against clickbait when we realize we aren't alone in this. I don't just mean that we aren't alone in the sense that other people are fighting too, rather that there is someone else literally and spiritually willing to fight *our* battle for us!

I've always loved what Philippians 4 says about this.

> [6] *Do not be anxious about anything, but in everything by prayer and supplication with thanksgiving let your requests be made known to God.* [7] *And the peace of God, which surpasses all understanding, will guard your hearts and your minds in Christ Jesus.* [8] *Finally, brothers, whatever is true, whatever is honorable, whatever is just, whatever is pure, whatever is lovely, whatever is commendable, if there is any excellence, if there is anything worthy of praise, think about these things. Philippians 4:6–8*

As famous as this verse is, my favorite part is the image of Jesus guarding our hearts and minds. God genuinely desires to fight on our behalf. This verse almost gives us specific marching orders. We make our requests known to God in a spirit of thanksgiving, and God takes on those requests as we remain focused on the things worthy of praise. It's clear to me that God is beckoning us, almost pleading with us, to cast our cares on Him because He cares for us (1 Peter 5:7).

But the most important part of that verse to me is its layout. The passage starts with a command: don't worry. It then tells us how to do that: position yourself in the posture of thankfulness, which is not an easy task when you feel like quitting.

So we position ourselves with thanksgiving, and then we simply ask God to take care of the thing causing us pain. God, the giver of all good gifts, gives us three: He handles our situation, He gives us His peace, and then He stands guard over our innermost being.

After all of that He gives us one more command, laying out what we should focus on. I know it may seem arbitrary to say we should focus on the good, because if we could do that naturally, we wouldn't find ourselves in this mess in the first place. But think of it this way: God levels the playing field for us. Like a coach with a new quarterback, He tells us to ignore the defense and focus on our footwork. This young quarterback is struggling to keep an eye on all the assignments of each player in his offense, plus his own assignment, while eleven other dudes are coming to take his head off. There's a lot to focus on! But a good coach comes and reminds him to focus on his footwork: take five steps back, make the read, step into your throw, and release.

In the same way, God tells us there is no reason to focus on the what-ifs, or our part in creating this whole mess, or how unfair it may be. Those are all genuine things to deal with, just like a quarterback should focus on the eleven guys coming at him. But focusing on his footwork gets him into his rhythm, and focusing on the things worthy of praise gets us into ours. It's not just a simplified focus, but an elevated focus. We look above all the noise and get into our rhythm!

The very fact that verse 8 lists what we should focus on tells us this: we have a focus problem, not a *problem* problem. If we're ever going to win this war for our minds, we are going to have to forgo tapping out and reach to our teammate to tag out. We elevate our focus and let God fight for us!

Does tagging out answer all our questions? Like, why would that happen to us? Or, why do we feel this way? Or, why won't those thoughts stop, even after we felt like they were gone? No. Tagging out doesn't mean the fight stops, it just means you're not the one doing the fighting. And isn't our fight better off in His hands anyway?

WHAT HURTS THE MOST

The sad part about mind games and the war with clickbait is most Christians don't realize they have a teammate. I'm not talking about a friend to help process life with, or a counselor, or some social media initiative that gets you to open up. I'm talking about an actual teammate. A God who wants to go to war for you. A God who wants to take on he who is coming against you. A God who wants to fight off the clickbait for you.

TAPPING OUT DOESN'T STOP THE PAIN; IT MAKES THE PAIN PERMANENT.

Not with you, *for* you.

If we don't know we have a teammate, then our end goal becomes simply ending the fight. Once we feel like winning is no longer in the cards, ending the fight becomes the goal. That's why tapping out is so appealing. That's why giving into the label or choosing to stay with the wrong person is so tempting: at least the fight is over.

But when someone taps out, they lose. The initial pain is gone, but a new pain starts settling in: the pain of the loss. They came to the ring with promise, and now they leave in defeat. Tapping out doesn't stop the pain; it makes the pain permanent. The actual fight didn't cause anything, but quitting did.

Think of a fighter who taps out in the midst of seemingly insurmountable odds. They believe the immediate pain will subside and assume that is the greater victory. So they tap out, only to find out the only true chance at victory just fell through their fingers. They watch as the other team parties. They see their fans, the people who believed in them, hit the exits full of

WE HAVE A FOCUS PROBLEM,
NOT A *PROBLEM* PROBLEM.

disappointment. All that pain is officially in vain. I'm sure, for a moment, they feel even worse than they did before they tapped out. Tapping out felt like the only option, but it actually robbed them of their options!

Quitting is what hurts the most! That's why we can't give in. We can't tap out! We can't believe lies, even if they do seem more concrete than the truth. We can't leave the church because we feel we'll be judged. We can't succumb to whatever lies about identity pop culture is adopting nowadays. We have to stay in the fight. We have to turn to our teammate and let God fight for us. It's the only way to win!

Staying with the wrong person, even when your family can't stand them, is actually not that appealing. The appealing part is not having to go back to the drawing board, going back to being single again. We feel like we'd be going back to a scary, lonely place. We don't know how many options we'd really have! But tapping out and choosing to stay with the wrong person is truly the *only* option that actually limits our options. If we honor God and step out in faith, then the Ephesians 3:20 nature of God goes to work. And now, every day is a day full of possibilities! Staying with the wrong person removes God's ability to answer His own promises.

Giving into a label, believing you are something counter to the biblical understanding of love and identity, is what actually puts you in a box—a box God did not create!

Choosing to leave the church after correction is what actually judges you. You've now made the decision; you are someone who leaves healthy things even when they get hard. The church didn't make that decision for you, even if they did handle the situation wrongly. But choosing to leave because they mishandled the situation tells everyone else that they have to handle everything perfectly around you, or else you'll leave them too. Is that the message we want to relay to our spouse, our kids, or our job?

I'm not passing judgment on anyone in these situations at all; it's actually the act of receiving the assumed judgment that judges them. And that's not my opinion at all, it's Scripture's: "For with the judgment you pronounce you will be judged, and with the measure you use it will be measured to you" (Matthew 7:2).

According to this verse, we create the standard of judgment. The judgment we walk in is actually our decision, just like tapping out is our decision. Tapping out is what ends the fight, which means the outcome of the fight is in our hands as long as we stay in the fight. And now that we know we have a teammate, we can stay in the fight while letting God fight for us! We elevate our focus and let Him take care of it!

This isn't even your fight! It never was. As we referenced Psalm 5:8–10 earlier, our enemy is in full out rebellion against God, not us. We aren't so gifted that the enemy is terrified and has us on some Most Wanted list. He isn't afraid of our calling being fulfilled. He's scared of God's plans being fulfilled. The enemy is not trying to end you—he's trying to avoid his own end!

This was, and is, God's fight. So let Him fight it! David believed some knowledge was too great for him (Psalm 139:6). Isaiah taught us that God's ways and thoughts kick ours in the face (Isaiah 55:8). If that's all true, tell me how the outcome of this battle with clickbait is better off in our hands?

Whenever you're tempted to tap out, to slap the canvas and give up, tag your teammate and get out! *Tag out*—don't tap out.

THE LESS I KNOW THE BETTER

Tagging out is hard, though, because it doesn't end the fight. Again, that's why we're so tempted to tap out. It ends the fight, or at least ends something.

We tend to believe there's peace on the other side of tapping out. I think that's why Eve tapped out. Her eating the fruit wasn't so much of a blatant distrust of the Father's instruction as it was a way of stopping the fight within herself. This fruit was from the tree of the knowledge of good and evil, which leads us to believe there were things she didn't know! And apparently, she wanted to know. Was God holding out on them? Could they be like God? She wouldn't know until she tried. She probably believed she would eat the fruit and finally know, and then she could have peace.

As absurd as this sounds on the surface, we have all fallen for this temptation. We all know how uncertainty can rob even the greatest paradise of its peace. We've all seen the enemy create inner turmoil in the midst of a physical paradise. Maybe, just maybe, Eve took the bait; she tapped out, believing there was peace in knowing.

Sadly, she was terribly wrong. "I will make your pains in childbearing very severe; with painful labor you will give birth to children. Your desire will be for your husband, and he will rule over you" (Genesis 3:16).

Eve quickly discovered staying in the fight was the less painful option.

We are all Eve. We all have believed the pain will stop if we tap out. And like Eve, we all realize that couldn't be farther from the truth.

I hope everyone reading this book hears this loud and clear: there is no victory on the other side of tapping out. There is no peace. The pain doesn't subside. There is no peace in *knowing*. Tapping out is actually the catalyst to more pain and inner turmoil! The mind games get worse. The clickbait becomes harder to identify. Finding your identity is a shot in the dark at a moving target. Tapping out turns paradise into a desert.

I HOPE EVERYONE READING THIS BOOK HEARS THIS LOUD AND CLEAR: THERE IS NO VICTORY ON THE OTHER SIDE OF TAPPING OUT.

Let's tag out!

Tagging out isn't simple by any means, but it's the only way to stay in the fight. It's the only way to combat clickbait. We've identified five major clickbaits that the enemy will throw at us in an attempt to get us to tap out and end the fight, but you aren't going to tap out! You'll keep going. You're going to let God fight for you!

In order to do that, we have to discuss the truth behind tagging out. Unfortunately, like we already said, tagging out does mean there is still a fight going on. And even more unfortunately, our current struggle is not the only fight we'll ever experience. We will have to choose to tag out each and every time we find ourselves in the middle of the ring ready to tap out. That's why the antidote to all this clickbait is a continual decision to let God do the fighting all while we focus on the things worthy of praise.

Fighting the war with clickbait and refusing to tap out will require things we have to consistently do over time. The four truths we'll be discussing in the following chapters to fight this war will seem like they are the one-stop shop of answers, but they are not. Combined with the pursuit of time with God and the study of His word, they will each be part of the answer for part of the time. Having a healthy thought life is like having a healthy physical life; it's not two months of eating healthy and you're good to go. It's the consistent commitment to healthy habits in your diet paired with a consistent exercise routine.

Consider a car. A car needs four tires working in unison in order for all the technology on the inside to actually matter. One tire does a car no good! Heck, even three tires won't get you anywhere worth going. If one tire is off, it holds back the entire car. In the same way, we as Christians need all four of the components we'll discuss in the following chapters if we're going to combat clickbait over the long haul.

Like a car, you have so much value on the inside. You have calling and purpose, gifts and talents, and the very breath of God within you! But the motor in a car won't matter if the tires aren't working. Tires may not be the most expensive part of a car, but a car won't carry out its purpose without four working tires in unison.

So now that we've decided we will tag out and not tap out, let's look at these tires!

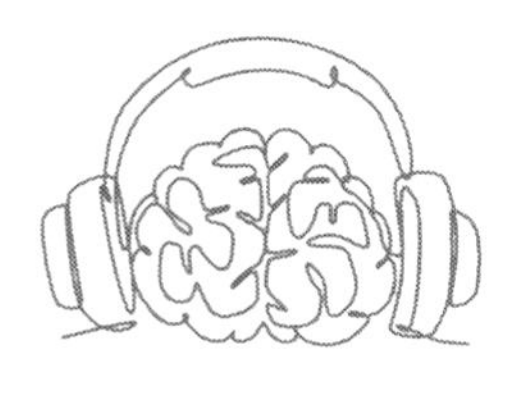

CHAPTER 9

"HOW THE TURN TABLES"

One of my favorite *The Office* quotes of all time comes as Michael is about to walk into a business meeting to discuss the purchase of his new paper company, the Michael Scott Paper Company. He walks up to his old office, looks David Wallace right in the face, and says, "Well, well, well . . . how the turn tables." It's a glorious moment of television. It's one of my favorites because we've all been there! We've all ruined a perfect moment fumbling over our words, but more importantly, we've all watched a situation completely turn on us.

Esther's story is one of the main Biblical examples of watching the tables get turned. Haman is the bad guy in this story, and he tricked the king into signing a decree to have all the Jews in the land killed. Oddly enough, the king had just married a Jew named Esther. Haman's plan goes south, though, and ends this way: "So they hanged Haman on the gallows that he had prepared for Mordecai" (Esther 7:10).

Oh, how the turn tables!

God took what the enemy meant for harm and used it for the good of His people. However, I think the real beauty in this story is robbed if you know the ending. We forget that Esther and Mordecai didn't know how the story would play out. It had a good end, but it also had a good beginning—until the tables turned.

In Esther chapter 2, we read all about God's favor on Esther and her uncle Mordecai as a result of their obedience. The story starts with King Ahasuerus, king over 127 provinces, looking for a wife. He starts a lavish competition to see who he will pick as a wife and eventual queen over all his provinces. Some scholars believe this process could have taken years before a woman was finally selected, and at the end, it was Esther chosen as the wife and queen. She watched as God's hand selected her out of thousands for this great honor!

I imagine her sitting around after the fact, basking in God's faithfulness. She went from rags to riches, literally. And then chapter 3 hits; the tables have turned.

All hell breaks loose, not just for Esther and her uncle, but for all the Jewish people. Mordecai had unveiled a plot by Haman, number two in the land, to kill every single Jew, including the king's new wife and her uncle. Once this decree went out, the Bible says the entire city was thrown into confusion. (Esther 3:15)

Imagine how Esther must have felt! Remember, she didn't know how her story would end. She didn't know God was having her enemy build up the gallows for his own demise. All she could see was what was right in front of her. Yesterday God blessed her with the marriage to the king, but today that favor went sour. She literally watched as yesterday's favor turned into today's nightmare. All that "favor" got her married to the man whose ring stamped the decree to kill her and her people.

We've all watched as yesterday's favor turned into today's pain. We've all watched the boss that promoted us turn to scrutinize us, we watched that job we prayed for become a very different subject of prayer, and we watch giants walk around every promised land. We've all watched the struggle come back, even after that great moment in church made us believe it was over and done with. We've all taken the plunge to leave everything we know for a land God will show us and ended up spending some time in the desert. We've watched God bring us Isaac after a lifetime of infertility, only to ask for him back a few years later.

I don't know what I would do if I were in Esther's position. I'd probably get caught up in how it happened, why it happened, and pray that it would unhappen. And I know I'm not alone! The temptation to tap out is always there; it's a very natural part of tagging out. Esther was tempted to behave this way too. But Esther shows us how to react in times when the tables have turned against us!

LIFE'S MAIN CHARACTER

I'm sure Esther wasn't a big fan of this part of her story. Not only has this decree gone out, risking the lives of all of her people, but she was in a hopeless place. Yes, the king was her husband, but it was their custom that only people summoned by the king would be able to approach him. Anyone that approached the king without being summoned would be put to death. Her husband had stamped a decree that allowed Haman to kill all the Jews, including her and her uncle, and she couldn't even go and speak to her husband about it.

I'm sure she wasn't very pleased with the God who sees the end from the beginning, the author and perfecter of her faith. I can't imagine the clickbait that came at her from all sides: the self-pity, the "maybes", the reminiscing, the offense, and the self-diagnosing. We've all been there! Like actors with a bad script, we've all wanted to argue with God over the plot. I don't think each moment of our lives is completely scripted with no room for free will, but we've all been angry with the director for how the scene is unfolding. We've all had a hard time seeing the necessity behind our struggle.

WE'VE ALL HAD A HARD TIME SEEING THE NECESSITY BEHIND OUR STRUGGLE.

But thankfully, good uncle Mordecai talked some sense into her.

> [13] *Then Mordecai told them to reply to Esther, "Do not think to yourself that in the king's palace you will escape any more than all the other Jews.* [14] *For if you keep silent at this time, relief and deliverance will rise for the Jews from another place, but you and your father's house will perish. And who knows whether you have not come to the kingdom for such a time as this?" Esther 4:13–14*

That's a loaded statement! And it gives us a lot to consider today. Note that her uncle and father figure helps her see that she doesn't get to play by different rules. *"Do not think to yourself that in the king's palace you will escape any more than all the other Jews.*" She may be the queen, but she too would perish if she didn't act now.

Sometimes we think we play by different rules than everyone else. It's definitely a subconscious thought playing a role in everything we do. We tend to think we're the main character of life, and the main character always wins in the end, right? But that thought process can lead to stagnancy, an attitude that says, "I'll be in my trailer!"

We then act like we'll somehow have another shot at life, treating it like a dress rehearsal. We act like we have time to wallow away in self-pity, offense, and everything else that trips us up. I believe this is what Uncle Mordecai was trying to get across to Esther. Even though her situation was difficult and speaking to the king was risky, they didn't have time to waste.

God has ultimately penned our story, but that doesn't make us the main character. We're not handed a script, a plot, and cast to just go through the motions. Instead, we take on similar attributes of God's creative ability; He is the potter and we are the clay (Jeremiah 18), but we also are a smaller potter with our own clay. We are handed the character and principles of God, and we can employ those things to create the life God has called us to live! I don't think we can somehow take advantage of God's character and principles, but I do believe we have a lot more power to shape our lives than we sometimes think.

In the midst of this great power, we find ourselves fighting with the director about the script. We don't like the last scene that took place, or the one we're currently in, and we fight with Him over why He's penned the story this way. But again, God did not use the analogy of a playwright when He spoke to Jeremiah; He used a potter. He uses the materials and shapes them into His final creation, and we can do the same with our current situation.

We have to live this way now! Like Uncle Mordecia said, we must realize we are shaping tomorrow and not fighting over yesterday. This mindset is a powerful weapon against clickbait and the desire to tap out. We are not helpless to what we are experiencing. We are victors, not victims. And we don't have time to waste. Maybe our current situation isn't as dire as Esther's. But like Esther, we've only got one life to live!

“We are victors, not victims.”

You won't get another chance to relive your twenties. You won't get another shot at doing things right. You've only got eighty years (on average) to honor God with your all, why waste a single one? Why waste a single moment being upset with the current plot when we have the ability to shape each and every moment from now on?

This is the first of the four tires we're going to look at: shaping tomorrow instead of fighting over yesterday. Throughout our lives, we will find ourselves in places we don't like. We will find ourselves in situations we didn't ask for. But each and every time, if we're going to make it over the long haul, we'll have to decide to put our eyes forward and press on. There's no time to waste in feeling sorry for ourselves or looking back to a simpler time. We only have one life to live! We must make the decision to keep moving forward regardless of what's coming against us. What other choice do we have?

It's simple, but it's true. Paul even says, "Brothers and sisters, I do not consider myself yet to have taken hold of it. But one thing I do: Forgetting what is behind and straining toward what is ahead, I press on toward the goal to win the prize for which God has called me heavenward in Christ Jesus" (Philippians 3:14).

This isn't about simply forgetting what is behind, but elevating our focus and looking ahead. It's choosing to take captive every thought that doesn't help us. Maybe your situation is unfair, but how does wallowing in that help you? Maybe you have wasted a lot of time, but how is wasting any more going to help you? We have to make the decision, right here and right now, to make continuing on our default option. What other choice do we have?

I love Esther's response to her uncle. She tells him, "Go, gather all the Jews to be found in Susa, and hold a fast on my behalf, and do not eat or drink for three days, night or day. I and my young women will also fast as you do. Then I will go to the king, though it is against the law, and if I perish, I perish" (Esther 4:13–16).

As bold as that is, she really didn't have a choice. If she didn't stand up, put her eyes forward, and take responsibility for shaping tomorrow, she would perish. Who cared if she put her life at risk? It was already at risk!

If I perish, I perish.

There is no dress rehearsal. There is no second shot. If you don't step up to the plate and fight off the enemy's clickbait, you will lose. And there won't be another shot. Let's elevate our focus and shape tomorrow!

SUCH A TIME AS THIS!

Uncle Mordecai's advice doesn't end there, as anyone who's heard this story knows from the really strong part of that passage. He stepped up to Esther in a time where fear was keeping her stagnant, and he said, "Who knows whether you have not come to the kingdom for such a time as this?"

Talk about an elevated focus. Esther was tempted to feel helpless, but her uncle showed her she was the only one who could help. She was tempted to ponder why God would put her in this situation, when in reality she should be thankful it happened to her.

Consider this for a second: what if the king was married to someone else who wasn't Jewish? Someone who didn't have an uncle Mordecai to talk some sense into her? The favor of God had to elevate her to this place yesterday so He could use her in it today. She was born for such a time as this!

Try to envision this story if Esther wasn't *exactly* where she was. What if Esther wasn't the one the king picked? What if somebody less Godly occupied that position? They probably wouldn't have pushed past custom, tradition, and everything else to save the Jewish people. Mordecai and thousands more would have died. And who knows the ramifications on Christ's lineage?

Esther stepped up to the plate. She made her way to the king, and he listened to her. She told him about the plot behind the scenes, and the king listened. Why would he listen to his wife? Because the favor of God was on her! The same favor that elevated her to the position of queen was on her as she pushed past custom and risked her life for her people. The same is true for you today; the same favor that put you here will get you through!

I know it's easy to look at everything coming against you and question, "Why me?!" But you should try to answer that question. Turn it around and ask, "What if it wasn't me?" What if someone less Godly had this happen to them? What if someone less in tune with the promises of God had lost their job, had their heart broken, or experienced loss?

Like Esther, you were born for such a time as this!

If you're facing something today, it's because only *you* could face it. We aren't the main characters of our story, but we do represent Him. If you're watching a lion come your way, it's only to train you for the future giants you'll slay. Those slain giants will bring glory to God, our main character. If you're promised a land with giants, it's only because the warrior within you is greater than the giants that stand against you.

This simple truth got Esther into the right mindset. She saw this problem as the real opportunity that it was, and she stepped into her rightful place, the place she was born for. In the same way, we must always elevate our focus to this place. We are born for this!

“

If you're facing something today, it's because only *you* could face it.

”

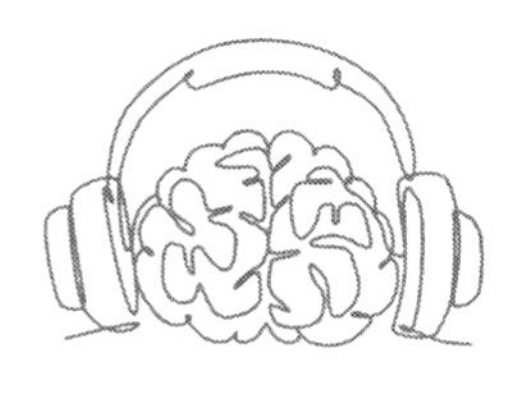

CHAPTER 10

"TRAIN FOR THE GAP"

When I was thirteen, I was finally getting the hang of tackle football. I was good at the throwing and catching portion of it, but I didn't enjoy the hitting part. But for some reason that summer, I decided to act like I liked the hitting part. And so, on the first day of practice, I made a mental shift to enjoy the hitting. To my surprise, it didn't hurt as bad as I thought! Of course, I was thirteen; the competition wasn't hitting all that hard anyway. But that didn't matter to me. I felt like I had turned a corner.

During the back half of that first practice, we ran wide receiver drills. Our position coach lined us up and threw us some passes. I ran my first hitch route to perfection; run five yards and then turn around and come back to the ball. And then of course, like clockwork, the ball hit my right pinky finger awkwardly. People heard the pop from all over the field. When all settled down, it looked like I had four knuckles on one finger.

They took me to the trainer and called my dad. I believed my finger was broken, but they believed it was just really badly jammed. For the next three weeks, my trainer did everything he could to fix what he believed to be a jammed pinky. Sadly—and I say sadly because I usually love to admit this—I was right. My finger was in fact broken, and we moved it and pressed it for three straight weeks.

By the time we finally went to the hand specialist, there wasn't much he could do. My finger was completely shattered. I still remember waking up in the surgery room as the doctor told my parents that he had done the best that he could. He told me I could try to go to physical therapy to get some of the movement in the joints back, but that it probably wouldn't do anything because he had to create a whole new joint toward the top of my pinky. I still can't bend it to this day!

Believe it or not, I don't blame the trainer or my dad for the lack of mobility in my finger; I blame myself. As the one in pain, I chose to listen to the trainer, and I chose to forgo therapy because the doctor said it was probably not worth it. Those were my decisions, not anyone else's.

In chapter 2 we discussed the four different types of voices we all have to balance in this fight against clickbait. From social media influencers, politicians, podcasters, celebrities and the like, it's never been harder to distinguish which voices we should listen to. In this ever-changing world, we have to realize one aspect of life has not changed: no matter how many voices are clamoring for your attention, you still are only held accountable for the ones you listen to, and we can put our head on our pillow in peace knowing that.

I know it may seem inconsequential, but knowing this is half the battle. We hit this point earlier, but we need to dive deeper as we discuss the second tire: we're only responsible for the voices we listen to. We see both sides of this truth in the Israelites' entry into the Promised Land.

In Numbers 13–14, Moses sends twelve men to spy out the Promised Land before they enter. Long story *very* short, we find out that ten of those men come back with a negative report, while Joshua and Caleb come back with a positive report. What most people know about this story is that they chose to not enter the Promised Land, and thus entered forty years of wandering in the desert. What gets lost in this story is how this choice was made.

It's easy to assume that these twelve men voted, and the ten negative reports outweighed the two positive reports. I assumed these men shared what they had found with Moses, and he ultimately made the decision to turn around. But that isn't what happened. Look at Numbers 14:1–5, which is right after the two spies shared what they had found:

> [1] *Then all the congregation raised a loud cry, and the people wept that night.* [2] *And all the people of Israel grumbled against Moses and Aaron. The whole congregation said to them, "Would that we had died in the land of Egypt! Or would that we had died in this wilderness!* [3] *Why is*

the Lord bringing us into this land, to fall by the sword? Our wives and our little ones will become a prey. Would it not be better for us to go back to Egypt?" [4] *And they said to one another, "Let us choose a leader and go back to Egypt." Numbers 14:1–4*

The real story is that the twelve men had gathered within the hearing of all the people, and the people heard. Numbers 14 continues the ugly story, and it only gets uglier. The people grumble against God and want new leaders and direction, but God does not allow us to decide who leads us. God placed Moses and Aaron, two imperfect yet *chosen* leaders, to lead them. When they grumble against their leaders, they grumble against God.

It was all downhill from there. The people chose who they would listen to, and they were held responsible for that choice.

I did say this story shows both sides of this truth, though, as Joshua and Caleb both got their credit for listening to the right voices (Joshua 1 and 14) and were the only two to walk into the Promised Land! Caleb was given the highest places in the entire Promised Land; Joshua was Moses protégé and eventual replacement. They were both blessed because they chose to listen to the right voices when everyone else listened to the wrong ones.

GAP TRAINING

I've always been annoyed by the story in Numbers 13 and 14. I listen from the perspective of someone that would have wanted to listen to Joshua and Caleb but would have been overruled by the mob. Why would I care about what these ten dudes said about a land God promised me? Why would I care about the opinion of spies? I imagine myself walking up to Moses and saying, "Don't you think we should send in a few warriors to get a second opinion? Can't we split up into two groups: those that want to go in, and those that don't?"

I find myself having sympathy for whoever that guy is in that crowd, because it's unfair!

I imagine this guy watching as the twelve spies walked into the gap between the people and the Promised Land. I imagine him watching them come back, probably so overwhelmingly excited that this actually could be happening. Then I imagine him staring at that same gap, only watching it get bigger as they walk away.

We all have gaps between where we're at and where we want to be. We all have gaps between what we're experiencing right now and what God says we could be experiencing! And we don't know what we don't know, so we will all have to send someone who knows a little bit more into that gap.

If there's a gap between my sink and a working sink, I call a plumber to fill that gap. If there's a gap between me and the healthiest version of myself, I have to let a trainer, nutritionist, or doctor fill that gap. And in each and every scenario, I will live or die based on the person that I choose to fill that gap. George Lopez tells a joke about his uncle who has had to go to the bathroom frequently in the middle of the night for fifteen years. His wife finally tells him to go to the doctor, where he finds out he has had prostate cancer.

Then his uncle turns to his wife and says, "You make me go to the doctor, and now I have prostate cancer!"

The joke shows the severity of this truth: we are at the mercy of the people who fill those gaps. We don't know we have something until a doctor tells us, and once he does tell us, we absolutely believe it. We don't know what's wrong with our car until a mechanic tells us, and we end up paying ridiculous prices so things we didn't know were broken (and have never heard of) can get fixed. We're at the mercy of the people who fill those gaps!

WE ALL HAVE GAPS BETWEEN WHERE WE'RE AT AND WHERE WE WANT TO BE.

We live and die on account of those who stand in the gap. We live with the consequences of their actions. We cannot control what they do, why they do it, or who they do it for. The only control we have in this matter is our choice of who will fill those gaps.

I'm not just talking about our right to vote. I'm not just talking about our boss. I'm talking about the voices we choose to listen to. I'm talking about the voices that we elevate to the place of truth. We can't control what they say on the news. We don't know what agenda celebrities, industry leaders, and the like serve. We can only control who we listen to.

We need some training on who we should be listening to. People are inclined to fill gaps incorrectly. The Israelites dismissed the opinions of two warriors like Caleb and Joshua. Even the Jews rejected Jesus because He didn't fit the particular gap they were searching for. They wanted someone to fill the gap between their experience here on earth and their desire for a Jewish nation, and so they expected a warrior. When Jesus came on the scene, He didn't fit many of their molds for an Earthly messiah, and so He was rejected. The woman at the well didn't realize who she was talking to and the spiritual gaps He wanted to fill for her. It becomes so painfully obvious that she needs some gap training that Jesus even says, "If you knew the gift of God, and who it is that is saying to you, 'Give me a drink,' you would have asked him, and he would have given you living water" (John 4:10).

She was missing it. She didn't know what voices she should be listening to. It wasn't until Jesus mentioned all six men that she had been pushing into the gaps of her experience that she realized she was talking to someone much more than a prophet. She, the Isrealites, and the Jews, just like many of us, needed gap training.

So let's look at a few rules for gap training so we can listen to the right voices!

Firstly, we can't send carnal people into spiritual gaps and expect good results. 2 Corinthians 10:4 (KJV) says, "For the weapons of our warfare are not carnal, but mighty through God to the pulling down of strong holds." If our fight isn't one of flesh and blood, we'd better be choosing fighters that understand their fight! For instance, politicians were never supposed to act like pastors, nor are pastors supposed to act like politicians. No matter how badly people seem to get this confused, we must always remember that politicians represent the voice of the people, while pastors represent the voice of God. Not that pastors are God or that they can speak *for* Him, but that God has chosen the vessels of prophets and pastors as His mouthpiece.

Sadly, people tend to expect more from politicians than pastors, or they expect their pastors to be politicians. If we don't like the opinion of our politicians, then we can choose not to vote for them again. But we tend to treat our pastors the same way. We should never leave a church because we don't agree with the opinion of our pastor—character or theological issues aside. People don't agree with every single opinion or decision their politicians make, and yet they still vote for them! We need to switch this up. Imagine what the church could do if its members unified behind their pastor as long as they lived up to their calling in theology and character.

Pastors should fill spiritual gaps, and politicians should fill carnal gaps.

Secondly, gaps should be filled by people who care more about getting it right than being right. We should be following people whose aim is to get life right, not people who walk around in an aura of how right they believe they are. The wrong voices try to say they are enough; they're the only voice you need. The right voices point you back to God. This is why 80 percent of all advice is garbage (and yes, I did make up this statistic). My job as a pastor isn't to tell you what to do, but to point you to the One who created you, to the one who is actively calling you, actively drawing near to you, and is intimately involved in your life. Anyone who cares more about being right than getting it right isn't a person worth following.

Even with these simple rules, knowing who to follow and what voices are the right voices is hard. I really didn't know if my finger was broken or jammed, so I just listened to the people around me. In the same way, many of us just listen to the people around us rather than really pursuing truth. But if we apply these rules, we have a better shot at the promised land!

SECOND BEST PIECE OF ADVICE

Aiming to find people who fulfill both of these rules seems like a daunting task. But we need not look any farther than the local church, the imperfect, full of human error, yet holy house of God.

In this battle against clickbait, we need to be a part of a good church with a good pastor. I know it may seem too simple, but just because it's easy to understand doesn't make it simple to carry out. Also, don't allow its simplicity to fool you: it's hard to stop a Christian who's submitted to good, Godly authority.

Finding a good pastor—a good, Godly authority—is what the second tire on our car is all about. I know it's not incredibly life-changing to say "you need a good pastor," but outside of accepting Christ as your savior,

ANYONE WHO CARES MORE ABOUT BEING RIGHT THAN GETTING IT RIGHT ISN'T A PERSON WORTH FOLLOWING.

I don't know if there's a better piece of advice than that. Nothing will point you to a healthy growth in your faith over time like healthy, Godly authority.

I have a pastor. My pastor has a pastor. That pastor has a pastor. This system doesn't speak to church structure as much as it speaks to Godly accountability; no one man should feel like they have God's voice completely figured out!

Sadly, a lot of people undervalue the role of Godly authority in their lives. They do so at their own peril. I'm not saying a good pastor is the be-all, end-all; as we've already discussed, one tire won't do a car any good. But it's hard to stay in the fight long enough to win without Godly authority. It's hard to keep an elevated focus and remember you're born for this time without an Uncle Mordecai! We're safer listening to the voice of our pastors, and it's sad that this wisdom is a hot take these days.

Hebrews 13:7 says, "Remember your leaders, those who spoke to you the word of God. Consider the outcome of their way of life, and imitate their faith." Yes, pastors are imperfect. Some have caused a ton of hurt. Some represent our faith and our churches poorly. But for every one of those, there are ten good pastors who truly love their people. We can't be like Elijah, feeling like we're the only ones while God has hidden away seven thousand. Maybe you've been hurt by a pastor, but I promise you that God is still working and speaking through His church leaders. Pastors are good, imperfect people who can be trusted. There is a pastor out there who can partner with you in this long-term battle against clickbait!

I understand that this doesn't apply to all pastors, but saying their imperfection disqualifies them from their duty is absurd! Consider Samuel's story with Eli.

> *Now the boy Samuel was ministering to the Lord in the presence of Eli. And the word of the Lord was rare in those days; there was no frequent vision. [2] At that time Eli, whose eyesight had begun to grow dim so that he could not see, was lying down in his own place. [3] The lamp of God had not yet gone out, and Samuel was lying down in the temple of the Lord, where the ark of God was. [4] Then the Lord called Samuel, and he said, "Here I am!" [5] and ran to Eli and said, "Here I am, for you called me." But he said, "I did*

not call; lie down again." So he went and lay down. [6] And the Lord called again, "Samuel!" and Samuel arose and went to Eli and said, "Here I am, for you called me." But he said, "I did not call, my son; lie down again." [7] Now Samuel did not yet know the Lord, and the word of the Lord had not yet been revealed to him. [8] And the Lord called Samuel again the third time. And he arose and went to Eli and said, "Here I am, for you called me." Then Eli perceived that the Lord was calling the boy. [9] Therefore Eli said to Samuel, "Go, lie down, and if he calls you, you shall say, 'Speak, Lord, for your servant hears.'" So Samuel went and lay down in his place. [10] And the Lord came and stood, calling as at other times, "Samuel! Samuel!" And Samuel said, "Speak, for your servant hears." 1 Samuel 3:1–10 (KJV)

We can pull some significant truths away from this story. Firstly, the Bible says the word of the Lord was rare, and with no frequent vision. God desired to speak to Samuel, even though the "church culture" of that day was pretty weak. Secondly, God used the very man who was leading the weak church culture to help Samuel discover the voice of God. An imperfect man of God still knew what the voice of God sounded like, and he was able to use that knowledge to point Samuel in the right direction.

But lastly, and this is the one that moves me the most: to Samuel, God's voice still sounded a lot like Eli.

Pastors aren't perfect, and they'll have to atone for their misdeeds just like everyone else. God tells Samuel in the following verses, 11–14, that Eli will have to atone for his misdeeds, and Samuel seemed to be the beneficiary of Eli having to atone for those sins. Samuel didn't miss out because his "pastor" was less than perfect, but he was given a chance to "take the reins." Why? Because he remained close to spiritual authority, even if it was imperfect.

I'm not saying to stay under a man or woman who abuses their spiritual authority, and I'm definitely not saying all pastors are created equal. What I am saying is this: the battle of clickbait is hard enough. Why fight it alone?

I've decided to err on the side of submission to Godly authority. I'm going to remember those that spoke the word of God to me. I hope you do too. It's hard to get anywhere worth going without someone who's been there before. It's hard to get a car far with a flat tire!

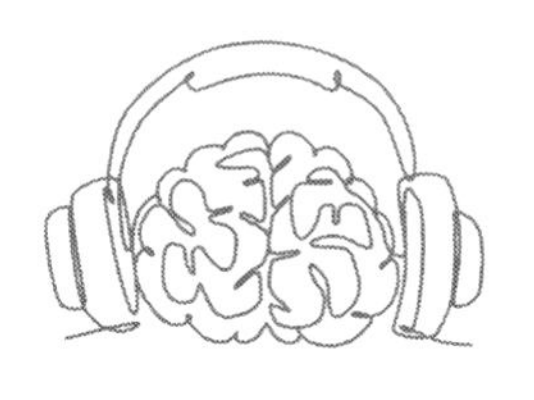

CHAPTER 11

THE VILLAGE NEEDS WALLS

Do you know what needs more maintenance than cars, boats, planes, computers, and just about everything else combined? People. Us. You and me. We need a lot of help, a lot of the time. We need constant upkeep. We need doctors, lawyers, friends, parents, pastors, teachers, mechanics, chefs, entertainers, developers of all kinds, and more. We literally need more than we can provide for ourselves.

That's why we're born into families, which are part of a community, which is part of a city, and part of a state, and so on. We are born into this massive choreographed song and dance of every person doing the little part that they can to help everyone else while they're being served by everyone else doing their little part. It's just life!

Our constant need for maintenance should relax us, not frustrate us. As much as we wish diet pills and quick fixes work, we all know they don't. They can't. You don't have just one thing wrong with you, and that's just today's needs! You'll have different ones tomorrow. It's why this portion of this book offering solutions is written in a more relaxed fashion; each of these last four chapters are only part of the answer, part of the time. Each of the four tires on our car of faith will need maintenance! You'll need other books, and other sermons, and more truth in order to get it all right.

When I started writing my first book, an author friend of mine gave me this great advice: simplify, simplify, simplify. He taught me to consolidate everything I'm trying to say in as few words as possible. Why waste time say lot word when few words do trick, right? (Yes, yet another *Office* reference!)

This is the mentality I take with me everywhere now. Whenever I'm developing a sermon, or reading a book, I'm mindful of how many words it takes to communicate a particular thought. That's why I was fascinated when I read some of Jordan Peterson's thoughts in his book *Beyond Order*. He talks about the value of community and how we exist among other people, not simply as individuals. He says:

> *If you begin to deviate from the straight and narrow path—if you begin to act improperly—people will react to your errors before they become too great, and cajole, laugh, tap, and criticize you back into place. They will raise an eyebrow, or smile (or not), or pay attention (or not). If other people can tolerate having you around, in other words, they will constantly remind you not to misbehave, and just as constantly call on you to be your best.*

I chuckled as I was reading it. I couldn't get the image of a church lobby out of my head! People helping you know how to and how not to behave? That's church! Anyone who grew up in church knows what I'm talking about. We all know the balance Jordan Peterson is talking about: the frustration that social interactions can produce, but the genuine appreciation for your immersion in the church community. We all have been laughed or tapped back into alignment with the straight and narrow. It takes a village!

I don't say that tongue in cheek, nor am I making fun of either Jordan Peterson's words or the church. I actually believe it's the greatest compliment to the church. Here this great scholar has devoted all of his time to developing thoughts about life, and this particular truth can be summed up this way: go to church, and stay in church!

I'm a church guy. I have always been a church guy. If I found the greatest restaurant in the world, you'd want me to tell you about it. Well, with everything so many of us have experienced in church, we'd be jerks to keep it all to ourselves. And so, the third tire is simply this: we need church.

LOW POWER MODE

"A Christian without a home church is a homeless Christian." This is one of my pastor's favorite sayings, but many people are rubbed the wrong way by it. We instead hear things like, "Church isn't the four walls, it's the people." That can sound so good. The idea that we would all rally together to *be* the church sounds so moving, so inspiring, that the gates of hell truly could not prevail against it!

But sadly, this isn't what most people mean when they say that. Their declaration of what church is isn't meant to give more value to the people part, it's meant to devalue the four walls part. I know there's a balance, but the importance of the brick-and-mortar church cannot be understated!

It's easy to see people treat this balancing act between being the church and going to church more like a pendulum than an actual balancing act; they feel one side has been valued too much that they have to eventually overcorrect for the sake of balance. They are degrading the value of the physical gathering place of the church for the sake of "balance."

But can we do that? What *is* the value of the physical gathering place? Does the village need walls?

And why would we have an issue with so many Christians—lifelong, newer, and soon-to-be—waking up early once a week, preparing themselves, gathering together, worshiping God collectively, hearing the Word of God preached, serving one another, and giving to God's house?

Paul has a lot to say on the matter. He says, "Let the word of Christ dwell in you richly, teaching and admonishing one another in all wisdom, singing psalms and hymns and spiritual songs, with thankfulness in your hearts to God" (Colossians 3:16).

And then Paul says. "Let us consider how to stir up one another to love and good works, not neglecting to meet together, as is the habit of some, but encouraging one another, and all the more as you see the Day drawing near" (Hebrews 10:24–25).

It's easy to focus on the "not neglecting" part, which is still important, but this verse in Hebrews tells us to devote time to thinking about how we can stir up one another in love and good works. When we look at the entire pie chart representing how our time is spent, some of it is supposed to be devoted to teaching and encouraging one another in the faith! We as Christians must be intentional about *other* people being encouraged by the Word, as serving others actually serves our own self.

Look at this proverb:

One gives freely, yet grows all the richer; another withholds what he should give, and only suffers want. Whoever brings blessing will be enriched, and one who waters will himself be watered. Proverbs 11:24–26

When we water others, we get watered. When we bless others, we are blessed. It is genuinely better to give than to receive!

However, "not neglecting" is a deep truth for us today. If you read between the lines, it doesn't say, "We can't meet unless you're here!" It says the individual should not neglect the gathering of the saints. When other Christians gather together to stir up one another in love, to encourage one another, to sing psalms and hymns and spiritual songs, you should be there! This part of the verse implies the party will go on without you. So why miss out?

We all know that if any rule is ever laid out on paper, it's because someone was breaking it. If the author of Hebrews felt the need to write "not neglecting," it's because some people needed to hear that. Some people were neglecting the gathering of the saints, and many people still need to hear that today because they are still neglecting it. They're like the people who live on low power mode; just charge your phone, dude!

WHEN WE BLESS OTHERS, WE ARE BLESSED.

Maybe that's you. Maybe you have a good reason! Maybe the church you like the most is too far away, or you're too busy, or you simply believe you don't need the church.

But consider this: sleep experts have taught us so much about setting our body up for a successful night of sleep. They tell us not to just lie around in our bed at times during the day, but to only get in bed when it's time to go to sleep. Apparently, our subconscious can't tell our brains that it's time to sleep if we're always lying around in bed. We actually have to trick our brains into thinking it's time to shut everything down once we get in bed.

They tell us to stop looking at our phones one hour before we go to bed so the blue light doesn't drain us of our melatonin. They tell us to set our room up for sleep, leaving nothing else on the to-do list except going to sleep. We need healthy sleep on a nightly basis if the deepest parts of us are ever going to reboot and recharge regularly. The value of good, deep sleep cannot be understated.

Now, if our bodies need so much help recharging, why wouldn't our spirits? Wouldn't they need even more? If our brains need to associate our bed with sleeping, and laying around not sleeping in the bed can ruin that association, how much more do our spirits need a physical environment to recharge? The prodigal son knew where to run to when he came to himself and realized he had made the wrong decision. When you and I honor the church, our spirits know where to go. Even more than that, those watching us will know where to go too.

The enemy works very hard to disconnect people from the church. He works overtime trying to get us to take the bait of offense and self-pity to get us to leave our homes and become homeless Christians. If he would work that hard at one thing, we should recognize the value in it!

CHURCH WORDS

If you have any church experience, you've probably heard this very famous verse referenced before. We've heard it in worship, sermons, team rallies, televangelists' lectures, and any other church-related setting. They're some of the most used church words you'll ever hear. It's a powerful verse that calls people to repentance and humility, promising healing not only for individuals, but for the land.

> *If my people who are called by my name humble themselves, and pray and seek my face and turn from their wicked ways, then I will hear from Heaven and will forgive their sin and heal their land.*

I've always heard this verse as a call to citywide (even worldwide) repentance. Every time I'd hear this verse, I'd find myself spiritually begging the world to turn from their ways and repent so God can heal our land. I'd imagine people from every nation finally turning to God. I'd envision telling my kids about how ugly the world was when I was a kid, and how blessed they are to be living in a healed land.

“

THE ENEMY WORKS VERY
HARD TO DISCONNECT PEOPLE
FROM THE CHURCH.

If you were to ask most people where that verse is, they would probably assume one of the books of Prophecy. They'd assume Isaiah, Jeremiah, or Ezekiel penned these famous church words. Maybe they'd set the stage this way: the Israelites rebel and experience sickness in their land. So God gives his prophet a "thus saith the Lord" to draw His people back. The great prophet steps up and declares these incredibly powerful words and watches as the people hit their knees in repentance.

Or maybe they'd naturally assume it was a New Testament verse. Maybe they'd assume it was written in red, from the very mouth of Jesus, since it has a lighter, more grace-filled tone than some other verses we've read. Maybe they think this verse would come from one of the apostles preaching via letter to one of the many churches. These are definitely the type of scenes I imagined whenever I'd hear this verse in church.

But to my surprise, I recently discovered 2 Chronicles to be the rightful home of this verse. 1st and 2nd Chronicles are appropriately named, as they literally chronicle the events that took place during that time. This may seem like insignificant context, of course, until you realize that 2 Chronicles is laying out the history of God's first temple—His first church.

Let's set the appropriate scene for such incredibly deep words.

King David wanted to build God a house here on earth, and his son Solomon made it happen. Chapter 7 discusses the completion of God's first earthly home, and verses 11–16 gives us insight to its ribbon cutting ceremony.

> [11] *Thus Solomon finished the house of the Lord and the king's house. All that Solomon had planned to do in the house of the Lord and in his own house he successfully accomplished.* [12] *Then the Lord appeared to Solomon in the night and said to him: "I have heard your prayer and have chosen this place for myself as a house of sacrifice.* [13] *When I shut up the heavens so that there is no rain, or command the locust to devour the land, or send pestilence among my people,* [14] ***if my people who are called by my name humble themselves, and pray and seek my face and turn from their wicked ways, then I will hear from heaven and will forgive their sin***

> ***and heal their land.*** *[15] Now my eyes will be open and my ears attentive to the prayer that is made in this place. [16] For now I have chosen and consecrated this house that my name may be there forever. My eyes and my heart will be there for all time."* 2 Chronicles 7:11–16

I have to admit, finding verse 14 in the middle of this story blew my mind. I find it fascinating that God waited until the completion of the House to choose it for Himself. He has chosen a physical house for His Spirit to dwell. He even says He will have open eyes and ears to the prayers made in this place where His Spirit dwells. Essentially, as I take on the ridiculous challenge of trying to paraphrase God, He's saying, "I have decided to honor this house, and I will honor those who honor this house."

I'm not attempting to take away the value of the individual prayer or make it seem like the prayer in church is the only prayer worthy of God's ears. I believe the exact opposite of that! But I also believe part of the pie chart that is the Christian faith is honoring the house that God has decided to honor. If God calls it holy, then we too should call it holy.

> IF WE HONOR GOD'S HOUSE, HE WILL HONOR OUR HOUSE!

In this battle against clickbait, we cannot lessen the value of the local church. We cannot dishonor what God has decided to honor. Look at what the book of Acts says: "Pay careful attention to yourselves and to all the flock, in which the Holy Spirit has made you overseers, to care for the church of God, which he obtained with his own blood" (Acts 20:28).

Jesus obtained the church of God with His own blood. He gave Himself up for the church. If Jesus was willing to obtain the church with His blood, we should honor it!

We could get into the weeds of what makes a church a good one, when you should leave a church and when you should stay, but we'll save that conversation for another book. What's most important is understanding that you won't go very far without a good church. If we honor God's house, He will honor our house!

HUMBLE PIE

You may be thinking that the answer to God healing our land is a different president, or turning off the news, or even going old-school and destroying the internet altogether! But it's actually even more old-school than that. It's going all the way back to 2 Chronicles and honoring God's house.

We've established a consistent theme of identifying difficult problems with seemingly simple answers. I know most people would envision Captain Obvious walking into the shot when you hear me say that we can combat the incredibly difficult battle with clickbait by honoring church. It seems way too simple, but maybe it's not the act of honoring church that is difficult. Maybe it's the step before the first step.

Consider that, according to 2 Chronicles 7, this simple call to honor church requires us to humble ourselves. This sounds so simple, it's almost impossible to accept. But we sometimes reject cliches because of their simplicity and end up missing out on the age-old wisdom they carry. The truth in humbling ourselves is revealed by how many people feel they "don't need" church, since people who go to church do so because they know they need it. The ones who go to church for the long haul continually recognize their need for it. To understand your needs is to understand that you *have* needs, which is humility in a nutshell. We can't truly value God's house and His church without recognizing our need for Him and our need for His house. That takes true humility.

This type of humility, recognizing yourself as a being with needs, is tough. This isn't the kind of humility that aims to combat cockiness. But as soon as we recognize our needs, we immediately take the seat behind He that has no needs. And the revelation that someone who doesn't need anything is technically better off than someone who needs something instantly puts God in the driver seat and us in the passenger seat. Through the simple act of recognizing we have needs, we step out of the ring and tag our partner, and He hops in, ready to fight our battles.

And it's okay to have needs. Gifts wouldn't be anything of value if the person receiving the gift didn't have a need. I'll never forget the day I walked into church empty-handed when a friend of mine walked up to me and handed me a 1995 Dan Marino trading card. If you know me, then you know this is one of the greatest gifts I could ever be given. I wasn't expecting it at all! I walked into church expecting nothing but left with something amazing in my hands.

This is what happens in church every single day. People walk in left and right, not really expecting anything, only to leave with a tangible gift from God. They walk in without direction and leave with vision. They march in with fear and leave with peace. They walk in feeling low and leave with their head held high. This is the church that Jesus obtained with His blood.

This is why honoring God's church will heal our land. When we all collectively take our rightful seat, when we consistently go to church, we place God in His rightful seat. When we consistently take our rightful seat, we get out of God's way as He draws all men near to Him. As all men are drawn to Him, our land will heal!

I feel the need to reiterate: we will *never* end the war on clickbait, at least not while we walk the Earth. It is not a TKO type of fight, so it will never end with a TKO on either side. It's a slow burn. It's a lifelong, twelve-round type of fight. If we're ever going to tag out and remain out, we will need the consistent humility that serving God's house brings!

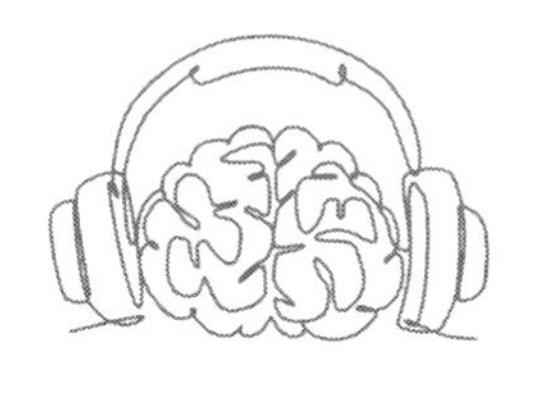

CHAPTER 12

ONE MUDDY WALK

I always admire people who make it to the end of a book. Thank you for being here. So far we've tackled all the clickbaits that we'll have to face, we've acknowledged the many voices we'll have to sift through, and we've aimed for tagging out, not tapping out. We've hit three of the four tires we'll need to maintain regularly in order to move forward in our car of faith: an elevated focus, a good pastor, and a good church.

As we move into the final chapter, I'm drawn back to the imagery of a car. Any car owner knows that accidents happen. Freak accidents happen. No matter how much you take care of your car, you will still get a nail in your tire. Someone rear-ends you. There are transmission issues, engine issues, sensor issues, and so much more. And it always seems to happen at the worst possible time in the worst possible place too. It always happens when you're already late to work, you just got bad news, it's ninety-five degrees outside, and you were already waiting for your next paycheck before you could even get groceries.

This happens in our spiritual life all the time. Our enemy throws clickbait at us left and right, again and again, and sometimes we genuinely don't see it. We might not even see it after reading this book. It also should be noted that our battle with clickbait isn't our only battle in life. We have so many things coming at us all the time, and sometimes one of our tires gets flat without any explanation. This is why our last and final truth is so imperative and would probably be the one thing I'd want anyone reading this to remember.

Sometimes you just have to move forward even when you don't want to. You'll have to move forward when you don't know why, when you were blatantly wrong, and when nothing makes sense. We have to act like there is a way out even when there isn't one. We have to learn to be content in the desert, call for rain in a drought, and choose joy in the pain. We have to pick ourselves up off the mat after every blindside hit, even when we thought we had tagged out. We have to choose to let God take care of it even when we don't understand.

We will all have to take a muddy walk every once in a while.

SAVAGE JESUS

One of the worst things about the modern day, nonspiritual clickbait culture is all the posts claiming someone "destroyed" someone else. It's all one "savage" moment after another. But when you actually watch one of these savage moments, they're hardly ever satisfying. They never live up to the hype. No one really destroys anyone. Even the moments that are pretty savage are most likely scripted.

I was watching a video about a thirty-two-year-old amateur basketball player. The post, and his entire page, was all about how good he was at basketball. Other pages had picked up this guy's posts and were promoting them all over the place because his moves were making people look silly. He was "savage" out on the court—until I started looking at who he was playing with. Every video was with young adults, probably eighteen to twenty years old, none of which looked like they were supremely talented at basketball. He wasn't playing with anyone at his level at all. He was picking on lesser players!

Those moves aren't very "savage," if you ask me. They're just sad.

John 9 actually details a truly savage moment on account of Jesus. I'm not trying to be sacrilegious, inappropriate, or culturally relevant at all. I genuinely think it's a savage moment, especially compared to His other miracles. See for yourself:

As he passed by, he saw a man blind from birth. [2] And his disciples asked him, "Rabbi, who sinned, this man or his parents, that he was

“

Sometimes you just have to move forward even when you don't want to.

”

born blind?" [3] *Jesus answered, "It was not that this man sinned, or his parents, but that the works of God might be displayed in him.* [4] *We must work the works of him who sent me while it is day; night is coming, when no one can work.* [5] *As long as I am in the world, I am the light of the world."* [6] *Having said these things, he spit on the ground and made mud with the saliva. Then he anointed the man's eyes with the mud* [7] *and said to him, "Go, wash in the pool of Siloam" (which means Sent). So he went and washed and came back seeing. John 9:1–7*

You don't have to search very far to see why I'd call this savage. Here Jesus is talking to a man blind from birth, and He decides to spit on the ground and put mud in his eyes. Can you imagine watching Jesus put mud in a blind guy's eyes? He's already blind! And then, with mud in his already blind eyes, Jesus sends him on a walk to get his healing.

This becomes even more outrageous when you consider all the other miracles Christ did.

- He healed a leper on the spot in Mark 1:40–45.
- He healed the centurion's servant who was still back at home in Matthew 8:5–13.
- He immediately raised a widow's dead son as he was being carried out into the streets in Luke 7:11–18.
- He told the paralytic to get up and walk in Matthew 9:1–8, and he did.
- The woman with the issue of blood was healed just by touching his cloak, and then He went to the house of a ruler to heal his daughter in Matthew 9:18–26.
- He touched two blind men and restored their sight in Matthew 9:27–31.
- He healed a mute man just by touching him in Matthew 9:32–33.
- He healed the invalid in John 5:1–9 by telling him to get up and walk.

There are almost too many examples to list, but to sum it up, Christ healed a lot of people immediately in His presence. When I compare the situation of the blind man with the mud in his eyes to the countless others listed above, it's hard not to feel incredibly sorry for him. We see that Jesus healed other blind people immediately just by touching them! Why was this man any different? Why did Jesus put mud in this blind man's eyes?

I know this passage sums the next part of the story up in nine words: "So he went and washed and came back seeing." But come on, that must have been a tough walk. He already couldn't see, and now he's being sent to find the pool. I wonder if he wanted to rub some of the mud out of his eyes. I wonder if he stumbled, or tripped, or bumped into anyone. I wonder what he must have been thinking—probably a mix of faith and hope for a miracle with a hint of feeling utterly ridiculous.

I'm sure he would have heard an example or two of Jesus's other, more immediate miracles. What made him different? Why didn't he get his healing immediately? I wonder if he felt the same emotions as the Israelites did in Exodus, who wondered why God would even take them out of Egypt just to let them die in the desert.

I'm not trying to add to this story for dramatic effect. I'm just trying to put myself in his shoes because I've been in his shoes already, and you have too. We've all had to take a walk with mud in our blind eyes, and we'll take one again. You'll have days where something just isn't adding up. You'll have days where all the hints and practices listed in this book just won't work. You'll have days where all four tires are fine, but something else is malfunctioning and you just can't figure out what it is. You'll have full seasons where you're robbed of all understanding.

It's in those moments, those worst moments, when we'll have to remember the blind man who took a walk with mud in his eyes.

We'll have to listen to that old Fred Astaire song: "Just put one foot in front of the other, and soon you'll be walking out the door!"

FINALLY KNOWING WHY

The more I read the story of the blind man with mud in his eyes, the more the disciples frustrate me.

This guy was just sitting around on a normal day when the disciples got curious. They wanted to know what would cause his blindness. They had a few theories, and they wanted to get a straight answer from Jesus.

I've had to check back to the passages a few times, only because the way they worded the question made it seem like one of the traps the Pharisees tried to set for Jesus. They had a question, and they wanted to get a lesson out of Jesus. I'm sure they weren't expecting Jesus to make an object lesson out of it, though.

I wrestled with a few questions of my own because of this story. Then it hit me. The disciples had a simple question, so the passage has a simple answer. This story deals with *why*.

> *As he passed by, he saw a man blind from birth. [2] And his disciples asked him, "Rabbi, who sinned, this man or his parents, that he was born blind?" John 9:1–2*

In the disciples' minds, and in our minds, "why" is complex. They thought this moment had a rich backstory, a root that had caused this fruit, and wanted Jesus to reveal it to them. They assumed it had to be something in the past.

Something from yesterday has caused today's struggle, right? However, is it always this simple?

Whenever we're in a muddy season, taking a walk with mud in our blind eyes, we too want to know what we've done to cause it, or what someone else did to cause it! We have to assume something, or someone, caused this unfortunate scenario; and we could move forward if we just knew what and why.

It's completely natural to ask why in these situations, just like it was completely natural for the disciples to ask their questions. But look at verse 2 again. And again. And again. Do you see the disciples asking Jesus if this guy somehow caused the blindness he was *born* with? This question doesn't make any sense at all! How could he have sinned and cause himself to be blind before he was even born?

To think something in your past, or your parents' pasts, can force you to take this muddy walk just simply isn't accurate. Our why questions deal with issues of the past, but Christ's answer to the disciples why question ignores the past altogether. Look at His answer: "It was not that this man sinned, or his parents, but that the works of God might be displayed in him" (John 9:3).

We deal with a why tied to our past, but Jesus deals with a why that pulls us into our future. Jesus told the disciples that God was currently doing (present and future tense) a work in this man! Yes, he needed to be blind from birth so the disciples would ask the question.

Some things from our past had to happen in order for our own moment to unfold. But muddy walks don't pull us back into our past, they propel us into our future!

This may not seem like a very detailed answer, but it speaks volumes. Even in its simplicity, doesn't it hit you like a ton of bricks? "Why did this have to happen?" Simply because God wants to use it. Because God wants to do something in and through it. Because He is in the business of restoration, redemption, and salvation.

Why? Because He is good!

This man's story became a bulletin board for everyone with questions. Sometimes we just have to take a walk with mud in our eyes even when we're blind. Why? Because God wants to show off. Because He wants to use it. He wants to do something in you and through you. In this life, you *will* have to take a muddy walk. You will have to do something without understanding why. You will have to take a walk toward getting better before you start to feel better. You will have to move forward and take that sacrificial climb up the mountain trusting that God will meet you with a ram at the top.

The passage tells us the pool of Siloam means "sent," which should encourage us today because we will all have to take that muddy walk. Whenever you're on one, it's not because you took a wrong turn. You were sent there!

HINDSIGHT IS 20/20

One of the craziest parts of this story is the last four words. He came back seeing! I really wonder what that guy must have felt when he opened his eyes and he realized how far he went as a blind man with mud in his eyes. He would have seen the spot where he sat for his entire life. He would have seen the exact spot where Christ would have put mud in his eyes, and he would have seen just how far he could go with a simple command: "Go."

Since hindsight is 20/20, sometimes you've got to get through the walk so you can look back and see through it all. God lets us move forward, completely blind with mud in our eyes, so we can get there and see just how far His word took us. God's grace is both forgiving and sustaining, and we need to be reminded of just how much He can sustain us from time to time.

I hope this truth gives you that little bit of gas you need to keep going, even when everything else from this book doesn't seem to be enough. Whenever you're tempted to tap out and submit to this battle with the enemy's clickbait, I hope you see the blind man taking a walk with mud in his eyes and it encourages you to take your own. And when you do finally open your eyes, I think you'll be shocked at how far His word took you. You'll be glad you tagged out and never tapped out.

GOD'S GRACE IS BOTH FORGIVING AND SUSTAINING

So to summarize everything: Elevate your focus today. You were born for such a time as this. You have what you need to be everything God has called you to be. You are not what your thoughts tell you you are, you are who God says you are. Find a good pastor, and stay close. Join the church, go to church, be the church, serve the church. And even when you're doing all that, and the voices get louder, let God pull you into your future with a blind walk with mud in your eyes.

You'll be shocked at how far His word can take you!

ACKNOWLEDGMENTS

To my wife, Richelle. Thank you for listening to me read every single chapter out loud multiple times to get the feel right. I am so appreciative of your unbelievable patience and support!

To my dad, thank you for everything. Just everything. Thanks for pushing me to be my best at every turn.

To my mom, I don't think I'd have this much to say if it wasn't for our talks.

To my sisters (and now brother-in-law), my greatest supporters from the beginning. You are truly my best friends. Thank you!

And to my grandmothers, the genuine linchpins of the legacy of faith that we all operate in. I'm the luckiest grandson in the world.

ABOUT THE AUTHOR

Christopher J. Alessi was born and raised in the beautiful and diverse city of Miami, Florida. He earned his Bachelor's Degree in Psychology with a Minor in Leadership Communication at Florida International University, and is pursuing his MBA in Theological Studies at Liberty University. He started serving in ministry in 2011 as a youth minister, moving to the young adult ministry of Metro Life Church in 2015. He presently serves as the Campus Pastor of the Doral Campus at Metro Life Church, and as a liaison to the staff. His desire is that all people would recognize the true Ephesians 3:20 nature of God and inspire others to do the same. Christopher serves in ministry alongside his wife Richelle, his parents Pastors Steve and Mary, and his three young adult sisters, Stephanie, Lauren, and Gabrielle, and his brother-in-law Christopher Muina.

Made in United States
Orlando, FL
13 September 2022